The *New* Normal

7 THINGS TO KNOW AS YOU
CARE FOR & LOVE A
CHILD WITH SPECIAL NEEDS

The *New* Normal

7 THINGS TO KNOW AS YOU CARE FOR & LOVE A CHILD WITH SPECIAL NEEDS

NANCY MUSARRA, Ph.D.

with her daughter, Giana

Foreword by Beth and Tom Tupa
Veteran NFL Family and Founders of App2Tapp

The Center for Behavioral Health and Sport Performance, LLC
6900 Granger Road, Suite #203,
Independence, Ohio 44131
(440) 584-0070
nancymusarra@drnancymusarra.com
www.drnancymusarra.com

FIRST EDITION

Edited by Michael Cioffi

Original layout by Courtney Fitzpatrick Huth

Cover design and final layout by Christopher DiAlfredi

Library of Congress Cataloging-in-Publication Data has been applied for.

ISBN 978-1515101819

10 9 8 7 6 5 4 3 2 1

To my parents, Helena and Bob, who are adorably optimistic, happy and kind. They've provided countless examples of how to laugh and enjoy life, love with a pure heart, learn with an open mind, think with common sense, and stand up for what you believe—without being afraid to stand alone.

Contents

Foreword

"*The New Normal* isn't just a resource for people who have children with special needs. It's a must-read for anyone who wants to live a full life."

Discovering how dozens of families have turned challenging situations into positive, even inspiring, experiences is what makes *The New Normal* so intriguing. Nancy's collection of real-life stories can resonate with anyone. We all experience tough times; it's just a matter of degree.

Timmy, our second son, was born with gastroschisis, a birth defect of the abdominal wall. During the pregnancy, we were told that we could be in for a long haul of problems with our new little guy. Timmy was premature and, only two hours after his birth, had surgery to repair his abdominal wall.

By the grace of God, we ended up with the best-case scenario. But we found ourselves on a path we had never traveled before. When he was very young, Timmy had two near-death experiences caused by RSV (respiratory syncytial virus)—once when he was 5 months old and again at 14 months. Both of these scary moments happened while Tom was away at training camp. This added to our worry and stress as we experienced an array of feelings, including horrible guilt.

There's a story in Nancy's book about two parents who battled the very same feelings. They were tormented by guilt, realizing how their two "normal" children would be affected by living with a sibling who would require a lot of attention. The story really hit home with us. Despite our initial struggle with guilt, we didn't share our feelings with one another. In fact, it took reading *The New Normal* for us to really talk about that experience. We realized that we were both feeling guilty and that others feel the same way.

Another story that hit home with us is about a mom who admitted she didn't bond with her child in the beginning because she was afraid of losing him. This story reminded us of how we felt after distancing ourselves emotionally from our child because we thought he was going to die. That story got us talking. Thank God we could let go of that burden, knowing others have felt the same way.

We smiled as we read the last chapter. This one is filled with stories of how children, just like ours, chose to embrace children with disabilities and establish real friendships. We are witnesses to our kids establishing friendships with Giana, Nancy's daughter with special needs.

Nancy has also raised two boys, both completely devoted to their sister. They love Giana so much that it's difficult to describe. They are natural leaders who, by example, teach others how easy it is to focus on the person, instead of the disability. We have watched our kids follow their lead as they established friendships with Giana and her friends.

Throughout our friendship, we have learned so much from Nancy, and we admire her positivity and resilience. And we love that Nancy makes sure her daughter has the same experiences her classmates have. When Giana attends football games, we watch as kids gravitate toward her in the student section. The students—and her brothers—cheer with her, involve her in the high-fives and make sure she's safe when the student section gets rowdy. We were thrilled to see Giana participating as the water girl for the varsity basketball team. We are proud of our kids for paving the way for other varsity players to get to know this wonderful person.

Remarkably, Giana's challenges and setbacks seem to give her mother more energy to move forward, focusing on everything Giana can do—amazingly well. Nothing seems to stop Giana from smiling, making us laugh and reminding us all to appreciate what God has given us this day.

In *The New Normal*, Nancy shares the perspectives of real parents, siblings, grandparents and friends, offering an unfiltered glimpse of life with a child who has special needs. The fears, frustrations and elation of these children's parents and loved ones can be felt through their words. Nancy's experiences with Giana—not as a doctor, but as a mother— have given her insight most of us will never have.

Along with powerful stories, the book is filled with tools that make us think about, acknowledge and shed light on our own experiences. As you read the "My Thoughts" box after nearly every story, you'll get a healthy dose of Nancy's realistic and proactive attitude.

Our friend's decision to share these stories and tools isn't because of her professional training. And it's certainly not because her life is easy. Nancy recognizes the impact her book can have on all kinds of people, many of whom have never known a child with special needs. This invaluable resource is a must-read.

As you begin to read, you'll soon find a story that reminds you of someone you know or perhaps evokes memories of your own story. One thing's for certain: it will be tough to find a story that won't tug at your heartstrings.

Anyone who knows a child like Giana understands that every day brings something new. It's a given that today isn't going to be like yesterday, and tomorrow won't be like today. It's essential to find a way to take the moment, the event, the setback, the accomplishment, and make it the best it can be. This book gives us the perspective to do exactly that.

Nancy, the psychologist, has a wonderful career that has helped her recognize the power of living life in a healthy, positive way. Nancy, the mother, provides the realization that life throws us curves. *The New Normal* offers an honest yet encouraging look at life. It's our hope that it helps you always keep your glass "half full."

—*Beth and Tom Tupa*

Acknowledgements

To the over 500 parents, caregivers, families, teachers, medical professionals and coaches who took the time to share their stories:

Thank you. I thank you for talking openly and honestly about what life is really like when no one's watching. It means the world to me that so many of you shared your thoughts, tears, laughs and joys about the New Normal that defines your journeys. Without you, there would be no book.

My hope is that, collectively, our stories will be a solid stepping-stone for new parents and caregivers who find themselves in our shoes. We certainly don't have all the answers. But together, we're the experts. And we share a lot of the same questions. As a strong and united group, we'll continue to search for answers and solutions that result in the best possible outcomes for our children.

To the brothers and sisters of children with special needs, I can't even begin to describe how important you all are in our lives. Listening to your stories, strengths, insights and perspectives was a privilege I'm so grateful to have had.

A very special thank you to my sons David and Bobby. There are no words to describe what it's like to watch you unconditionally love Giana. I love that I'm your mom.

I would like to express a heartfelt thank you to those individuals who are simply irreplaceable. You know who you are, especially if you've received a "Thanks for being awesome!" message from me. You're the wonderful people who make the conscious choice to be kind, inclusive and real friends to individuals with special needs. Your contagious acts of kindness don't go unnoticed.

I'd also like to say a huge thank you to my sisters, Nicki and Luann, as well as my best girlfriends, Joni and Jess, who are rock stars to me. You fill my life with fun, happy and spontaneous lifelong memories.

To my professional team, I thank you for your time and talents. Roman Jakubowycz and Eugene Shatsman (National Strategic Group), Michael Cioffi (Editor), Corey Fitzpatrick Huth (Corey Fitzpatrick Huth Photography & Graphics), Diane Van Nostran (DVN Photography) and Chris DiAlfredi (Eques). I appreciate your enthusiasm, guidance and professionalism as I navigated the world of publishing.

A big thanks to Tom and Beth Tupa for your friendship and kind words. I am truly blessed our paths crossed.

And lastly, I want to thank my hero,
GIANA NICOLENE.
There are times when I fall apart, but each time
you hug me, you put my pieces back together.

છ

Introduction

I WISH I HAD A BOOK like this one 17 years ago. It would have been a window through which I could have seen how others in my shoes reacted to unfamiliar—and sometimes scary—situations.

It's unsettling when you know something about your child isn't quite right. It's even more unsettling when your child, at any age, seems perfectly healthy and then unexpectedly develops a medical, emotional or physical illness—or is involved in a life-changing accident.

When I found myself in the first situation, two thoughts raced through my mind: *How do other parents and caregivers handle something so unimaginable? How do they maintain a life balance while thinking about and following through with tough decisions to best help their child?*

My little bundle of inspiration

I began writing this book in my head soon after my

daughter was born. Almost right away, I knew something wasn't right. But I wasn't certain until she was between eight and eleven months old. When she was just two months old, I couldn't figure out why her behaviors were so inconsistent throughout the day. One hour she seemed fine—like a typical baby—and then, a few hours later, she'd be crying or moaning in pain or staring off into space, unable to focus on faces, toys or sounds.

Throughout the first few months of her life, I consulted with our pediatrician and a number of emergency room doctors. And I asked family members and friends if they, too, sensed that something wasn't quite right.

During each doctor's observation, my daughter responded like a typical baby who may have been hungry, tired or agitated. The doctors concluded that she behaved normally for a child her age. Still, I was convinced that something wasn't right. Was she having problems hearing or seeing me? Or was I looking for something that simply didn't exist?

I started writing my observations in a notebook to see if there was some sort of pattern. I wrote down everything I could each day for the first four months of my little girl's life. I filled two notebooks. I found it difficult to focus on anything other than her, convinced that if something was wrong, I could figure it out and fix it.

As she continued to respond inconsistently, a new set of symptoms appeared in month four. She began experiencing hand and finger tremors, and sometimes she'd shake uncontrollably. It was frustrating to see a new problem emerge, but comforting to know that, this time, others noticed it too. Most of the time, she was calm and relatively comfortable.

But other times, her whole body would shake as if she were going to jump out of my arms. Doctors acknowledged the symptoms, but test results were negative. All we could do was continue to observe her.

When she was six months old, the symptoms I had recorded in the notebooks started to make sense. One night, as I picked her up, her body started to shake and stiffen. Her lips were pale blue and covered with foamy drool. Then, with her eyes rolled back, she had her first obvious seizure. I kept the shiny black patent leather shoes she wore that night so I'd remember how little she was when our journey began.

I'm told the first seizure is always terrifying to witness. I agree. However, looking back, the many seizures that followed were not any less terrible. Unfortunately, 17 years later, she still hasn't experienced one day without them.

The night of the first seizure was followed by many tests and trials with medications. It was discovered through video electroencephalogram (EEG) tests that she was having different types of seizures throughout the day and night, and that her brain functioned differently from a normal baby's. She had constant spikes, followed by slow brain waves after each discharge. Each spike recorded more than 40 extra electrical discharges per minute.

At the time, I knew very little about seizures and even less about the many different types that existed. I was equally unfamiliar with neurological terms such as spikes, waves, electric storm and vagus nerve stimulation (VNS). Although the terminology was new, one thing seemed constant. Every doctor, intern, nurse and technician agreed that the EEG pattern demonstrated on the monitor was way outside the normal range, even for those diagnosed with epilepsy.

As time went on, I became familiar with the names of medications and neurological tests. I also became accustomed to the surprised looks of the EEG technicians who were new to our situation. After connecting the leads to my baby's head and turning on the monitor, it wasn't unusual to hear the technician say, "There are so many discharges. Let me check to make sure the machine is working properly." Forcing a half-smile, I'd say, "It would be great if the machine were broken."

It never was.

I was assured that my daughter would have additional challenges. As a new parent of a child with special needs, I didn't know what to expect or whom I should contact to get the best help.

Watching my child feel miserable one minute and fine the next was a routine I'd grown used to. But now, I couldn't tell if her symptoms were caused by seizure activity or the side effects of her medications. Professionals couldn't be certain either. They could only observe her, evaluate her symptoms and adjust the medications based on today.

Medication adjustments were helpful, but temporary. Progress was slow, but at least it was possible. Predicting the future was less possible. No one knew what was in store for my little girl. They could only describe the possibilities. As I listened to various medical professionals describe the best- and worst-case scenarios, I felt scared and sick.

I felt sick to my stomach when told my little girl was ill and would have daily seizures, along with a host of other challenges. She was just months old and yet her life was filled with so many unknowns. I remember searching for a book or information about how other parents and caregivers managed these types of situations.

How do others find a balance when what to expect is unknown and the ups and downs are so inconsistent?

How do others think clearly when days and nights blend together and sleep seems impossible?

What can a new parent like me learn from the experiences of others who have been in this situation?

These questions brought this book to life.

Over several years, I conducted countless interviews with parents, caregivers, family members, friends, teachers and coaches, as well as with children who have special needs. I listened to the stories that defined their journeys. I started each interview by asking them what they would tell others who found themselves in this situation.

As I listened to their replies, seven things seemed to emerge over and over again. Equally important, all seven will help you better understand your child, his or her challenges and your roles as parent, caregiver and friend:

1. *Accepting the situation*

2. *Learning about yourself along the way*

3. *Understanding what your child can and can't do (yet)*

4. *Feeling alone*

5. *Addressing the situation as a couple*

6. *Responding to others and the shocking things they do or say*

7. *Embracing the good and those who care.*

A Shared Experience

This book isn't my story—it's *OUR* story. It's a thread in a tapestry of stories about children with special needs who are as similar as they are unique. As the parents of these amazing children, we've embarked on journeys that have required us to think beyond common sense and so far out of the box that we're often completely misunderstood.

Take comfort in knowing there are many more families who share our challenges. In fact, according to a 2008 survey conducted by the Health Resources and Services Administration, part of the U.S. Department of Health and Human Services, more than one-fifth of U.S. households with children have at least one child with special needs. That's approximately 14 percent of *all children* living in the United States.

It's my hope that reading about my experience, along with those interviewed, will encourage you to think about—and re-think—your own.

Sometimes we consider children with special needs to be gifts or blessings. Other times, we see our lives with these children as endless journeys paved with trepidation. Attitude and perspective shape our experiences for better or for worse.

When my daughter was eleven months old, I had a 2-year-old son who wanted to play all the time. And I was pregnant with a third. After my daughter's diagnosis, I spent months feeling numb, sorry and scared. I filled my head with questions, which made everything worse.

What kind of childhood or adult life was ahead of my baby girl?

Would she even live to be an adult?

What do I tell my two boys?

After torturing my mind with difficult, if not unanswerable, questions, I asked myself one more.

What kind of mom can I be?

I remember that day because I actually felt good. Once I asked and answered the "Mom" question, I was free to focus on what I COULD *do*.

I could organize my thoughts and observations. I could start finding professionals who could answer my questions. I could reject the notion of "can't do" and embrace the idea that she can. I certainly could decide to raise my expectations and refuse to accept the attitudes of others that would limit her possibilities. Once I defined my own "I can, she can" attitude, I felt a sense of freedom. I'd no longer ruminate on questions impossible to answer.

I started this stage of my journey by writing down two things to focus on each day. One: *I have a lot to learn.* And two: *She is my gift.* I still have the paper.

I named my gift Giana Nicolene.

Fast Forward

Now, 17 years later, she still has seizures and other significant challenges, but she's her own person. She knows what she likes, wants and dislikes, and why she's excited or disappointed. She speaks slowly and with a stutter. I learned to be patient and not finish her sentences. If she can work this hard to communicate, I can work even harder to listen. Her acts of kindness are many and pure. People gravitate to her. There's no possible way to exaggerate the emotional hell I'm in when my little girl suffers, or the intense joy and happiness

I feel when she tells jokes and stories, and explains her unique perspective of our world. Experiencing her is a gift. For those who know her, there's no need to explain. For those who don't, there's no easy way to explain. She has a way of living in the moment and lighting up the room with a feeling of happiness. Sure, she has challenges and problems, and she works hard every day to overcome them. But guess what?

She has more "no-problems" than problems.

She has no problem telling the truth, smiling each day and showing concern for others. She has no problem getting excited when others do well or feeling sorry when someone's hurting. She knows how to love.

My hope is that everyone, at some point, will meet at least one Giana. When you do, you'll understand what love really feels like and why being genuine, selfless and truthful matters if you truly want to get to know someone.

This book is a celebration of that epiphany.

Engaging and enlightening, children with special needs teach us to listen sensitively so we get to know the *person*, not the *disability*. In doing so, they help us to understand their world—and ours—from their perspective.

Finally, to all the people—scientists, medical researchers, doctors, pharmacists, engineers and other professionals—who work tirelessly to find cures for these disabilities, please keep searching for answers. Don't give up on us.

The *New* Normal

7 THINGS TO KNOW AS YOU CARE FOR & LOVE A CHILD WITH SPECIAL NEEDS

The New Normal

THERE ARE MILLIONS OF US. Throughout the United States and around the world, there are millions of moms, dads and caregivers doing their best to care for children with special needs.

Some parents are told their newborn most likely has cerebral palsy or some other genetic, developmental or physical challenge that may place the child at risk. Other parents seem to have a perfectly healthy baby at birth. Understandably, they're surprised when their child doesn't start to walk or talk at the "normal" age, or the child develops medical or emotional conditions that interfere with his or her development. Either way, millions of parents and caregivers find themselves trying to help children with disabilities they know almost nothing about. It's like solving one of those giant puzzles without being able to look at the picture on the box.

As I write this book, what's actually medically wrong with my teenage daughter is still a mystery. She's undergone years of testing and assessments. Like with many children who have special needs, her symptoms are difficult to diagnose and don't fit neatly into a specific category. I started noticing the symptoms when what I expected her to be doing at a certain age just wasn't happening.

Our children just seem to have more difficulty with language, eye contact, communication, balance, tolerating change, following directions, learning or behaving appropriately than other kids the same age. So what do you do when you sense something isn't quite right? Some parents raise their concerns immediately. They ask questions, scour the Internet for answers, write down their observations and ask others if they notice symptoms too. They seek professional opinions from a pediatrician or school staff members. Others choose to wait and see if their child grows out of it and starts developing like "normal" kids. It's hard to tell which approach is better.

We're flooded with confusing thoughts and emotions when our child has difficulties or is experiencing delays. It can be overwhelming to figure out what you should do, when should you ask questions and who can help.

The pressure can be intense when you're faced with important decisions about medications, implants, surgeries and invasive tests you know very little about.

Common sense reminds us that important decisions are the toughest ones to make. They require time for assessing and clarifying all the options. But when your child is hurting, he or she needs relief. One more day spent deciding what to do can seem like an eternity. Your child has waited and suffered long enough. Keep in mind the professionals can only help you decide among the best options.

The final decision is yours and yours alone.

I look back now at the decisions I've made a
that choices were never going to be clear, and ma
right decision was never going to be easy. Many interv.
treatments and medications are unreliable or temporary. Or
they only partially work. As some symptoms go away, others
may appear. The emotional highs and lows will continue. We
keep working the jigsaw puzzle, always focusing on what to
do next. The one thing we can count on to be consistent
in our lives is change. Change and challenges are normal in
the life of *every* child. Without challenges, they could never
learn skills to overcome or cope with adversity. Experiencing
change and difficulties helps children grow physically,
socially and emotionally. In many ways, what's true for *any*
child is true for a child with special needs. People outside
your situation may ask, "If change for any child is normal,
what's the difference whether the child has special needs or
not?"

Yes, change is normal for every child. But for a child with
special needs, it's a *different* normal.

Think of it this way. Most people naturally assume that
a 5-year-old who can walk and talk today will walk and talk
tomorrow. In our world, that's not always the case. It's very
possible that a child with special needs may walk and talk
today, but could find those skills challenging—or nonexistent
—tomorrow.

That's the difference. That's the New Normal. That's
what this book defines, explores and even embraces.

I couldn't have written this book alone. Luckily, I didn't
have to.

As you read on, you'll hear the voices of the many who have walked in your shoes. In these pages, they share their thoughts and experiences with an open heart and without holding back. Most of what they have to say is encouraging. And all of it's real. Unfortunately, reality isn't always comfortable or easy to hear. Touched by children with special needs, hundreds of moms, dads, caregivers, friends and family members share their emotionally charged stories. They've all been there, and they understand what it takes to be the best version of themselves while caring for a child with special needs.

Collectively, they're experts.

During my interviews, I learned about both the joys and the struggles that link their stories. These wonderfully real people talked, cried and laughed about the different ways they learned to cope with their situations. Although as individuals they cope differently, they're all bonded by their challenges, successes and the fact that they get it. They get how life has changed. They understand the New Normal and how a child with special needs can teach us a kind of love others can only imagine.

Their combined wisdom will show new parents what to expect and how to prepare as they deal with the daily challenges that come with caring for a child with special needs. The stories these people share are encouraging, if not inspiring. Collectively, their experiences form the foundation of the *Seven Things You Need to Know* to be prepared for *your* journey.

Your journey will be just as challenging, difficult and painful as it will be joyful, inspiring and enlightening. These seven must-knows center around what this journey teaches us about taking care of our children, our families and ourselves, as well as how to deal with the world around us. Only then can we achieve the best possible outcome.

1 Acceptance

DISABILITIES DO NOT DISCRIMINATE.

They can happen to any child for reasons known and unknown. Once discovered, life as we know it is forever changed. What we had envisioned for our lives, families and futures will be different. Not bad, just different.

When asked what was the most important first step of their journey, many parents and caregivers offered the same response: acceptance. Most explained that accepting the reality of their situation made everything else possible.

To anyone in this situation, the number of things to accept can seem endless. No one can tell you how or when your mind and heart will accept this reality. Only you know what it's like to walk in your shoes. Just remember, you're not alone. There are many of us who understand.

As one such person, I encourage you to read on.

"For as long as I could, I put off acknowledging that Joey couldn't hear a thing."

Theresa's Story:

"I remember my mother asking me if I thought Joey could hear. I felt angry and wondered how anyone could ask such a question. My response: 'Of course he can hear! What are you talking about?' But I knew. When Joey was a month old, I noticed he wasn't responding to sounds like my other children did. I remember testing him by standing across the room while I banged together pots and pans, hoping Joey would turn my way or cry from the loud noise. Sometimes he did, sometimes he didn't. Eleven months later, my husband suggested we both go to the pediatrician and ask her about Joey. Joey wasn't saying words or looking at us when we spoke to him. I was afraid.

I wanted to be with him during the testing and see for myself. The nurses tested him from across the room with a sound—not a vibration like I did at home with the pots and pans—and told us right then and there that our child was 'profoundly deaf,' removing any doubt that Joey had a severe hearing impairment.

I remember hating the terms they were using, but I knew they were right. I stood there and cried. I cried and cried, and didn't want to accept that Joey was deaf. I used to correct people when they referred to Joey as deaf and would say, 'No, he is hard of hearing.' I can't believe I used to correct the doctor and Joey's teachers. I must have sounded so silly or nasty at times, but I was trying to protect him. Now I can accept this. Yes, he's deaf. He really is. He basically can't hear a thing.

For me to accept this, I had to cry. That's just how I am. My crying worried my husband, who seemed to quickly accept my son's deafness. I asked my husband to just let me cry, and he respected that. I needed to go through all the feelings I had, including sadness, anger, disappointment and a terrible kind of fear. I cried for a few days, maybe weeks, almost nonstop. And then I was done. I usually cope that way. I let all my emotions out in the beginning and then I'm done. I was able to accept that Joey was different and that he was going to learn and experience this world differently.

Now, Joey's a teenager who's involved in school and sports. He gets along well with the others. We chose to get Joey cochlear implants. Along the way, we've found that decision to be both good and bad. You can still tell by Joey's speech that he has a significant hearing problem, but less so with the implants.

While Joey's peers accept him, some people who also are hearing impaired reject the notion of cochlear implants. Joey was surprised by some of the negative interactions he received because of the implants, and he feels shunned in some ways by the deaf community. We'll continue to deal with how Joey fits into the deaf community. We'll also continue to pay attention to how he interacts with people who can hear perfectly fine, as well as with those who wear implants. Overall, Joey's happy and active in school. And he plans to go to college like his sister and brothers."

My Thoughts: Allow yourself to experience your own unique rainbow of emotions, regardless of what they are or what anyone else has to say. Staying true to yourself allows you to stay connected with your courage.

"Time is different in our world."

Jackie's Story:

"I knew my life would change. But I had no idea that everything about what I did and how I did it would be altered almost 24 hours a day. I had been teaching third and fourth grade special education for five years before I had Tommy, my first child. I know many families who have children with special needs, so I understand the challenges of physical, academic and developmental disabilities.

At least I thought I did.

I quickly realized there was another perspective that only Tommy could help me to understand. I love my students, and the moment the kids left for the day, I got a break. I'd get to go home and relax, curl up with a magazine or do what I had to do around the house.

When I discovered my own child had special needs, I quickly realized there are no breaks. I had to accept that raising a child with special needs is 24 hours of dealing with situations you may have no idea how to deal with.

I knew something was wrong when he was a little boy.

Everything seemed fine until he was about 2 years old. He stopped interacting with us and seemed to retreat into his own world. He stopped talking and understanding things, and he seemed disinterested in the world around him. It was like something was missing one day, and it never came back. The more he regressed, the more I tried to help him.

One day, I realized being Tommy's mom was the most challenging role I would ever have. I had to adjust my work schedule, talk less on the phone and spend more time talking with teachers, figuring out how Tommy could learn. My husband accepted that my son was different. Unfortunately, he couldn't spend the time I could with Tommy because of his work schedule. I gradually accepted that how I spent my time had to change. I stopped planning lunch dates, shopping days, playgroup dates and summer camps. As Tommy grew older, it became harder for him to immerse himself in new situations. My son couldn't adapt to unfamiliar surroundings, so he'd be uncomfortable, a feeling that often would turn into frustration and irritation. I couldn't join my family and friends when they called me.

Tommy wouldn't even look at me. He'd scream in public. It was terrible. I felt a strong need to be with Tommy to help him develop a tolerance to new situations that seemed natural for other kids. I remember trying to explain to others that having a child was a 24-hour job. I became infuriated whenever others would say, 'Come on, Jackie. Every child is a 24-hour job. This is your first child, and you're experiencing what all mothers experience.'

Every time I'd hear that response, I'd say, 'Yes, I know every child is a 24-hour job.' What I said aloud would end there. But the thoughts inside my head continued. 'You don't get it. My 3-year-old doesn't look at me, doesn't say words, doesn't try new activities and is perfectly happy sitting in the kitchen corner for six hours playing with a spoon.'

I had to refocus and give Tommy the time he needed. I worked with him and got to know him. I helped him tolerate waiting, as well as new toys, sounds, smells and textures. I finally got him to say a couple of words. I'll never forget the day he looked right at me and said, 'Hi, Mom.' That was enough to motivate me for years to come. I knew I was doing something right.

Eventually, he got it, and I was able to get him ready to function at school by the first grade. By function, I mean he could sit in a chair with minimal rocking and humming. He could remind himself not to kick or poke the other kids at his table. He learned to write or draw pictures of what he was thinking instead of spontaneously shouting out his thoughts while the teacher was talking.

My time, schedule and whole life had changed. Tommy was often in his own world and perceived as a little brat instead of a child with special needs. He needed more time to fit into our world. I accepted that others couldn't understand my child's needs. I also accepted that I did, and that was all that mattered.

He's now 18 years old and a wonderful teenager. Tommy's close to family and friends who have come to understand him. They want to spend time with Tommy so they can get to know him, not just his disability. I'm proud of them and proud of him. And yes, he's different."

My Thoughts: Most of the time, we can't change the thoughts, feelings or perspectives of others. However, we can lead by example and support those who open their minds and hearts to our children and hope they follow our lead.

"I had to accept that I needed to learn everything and find the time to do it."

Jane's Story:

"In the beginning, I knew nothing about cerebral palsy. I wasn't a very good student, and I didn't enjoy school. But I needed to learn about cerebral palsy, a topic chosen for me when my son was diagnosed with it at birth. I had to become familiar with wheelchairs, ramps, prosthetics, physical therapy, surgeries, medications, pain management and anything else my son needed to live a happy life. I went to meetings and talked with other parents and individuals who knew about cerebral palsy or who had the same questions I had. I learned everything I could. The process is slow, and it takes patience to find resources that match your child's needs.

Looking back, I realize the time I spent learning about cerebral palsy and getting to know what my son really needed was worth every minute. We have three children in all, and our life is as unique as it is normal. We've all accepted the challenges of special needs in our own way. I think all my kids are more grateful for the good days since they understand the reality of a difficult one."

My Thoughts: We are all problem solvers to some degree. We either fix things ourselves or find someone who can. But on this journey, we learn to wait and accept that many problems or challenges are unclear and solutions may not come quickly or at all. Learning to stay patient and hopeful is universal to our group—another bond we share.

"I had to accept that I couldn't solve every problem today."

Christina's Story:

"I'm an engineer. I always strive to be better at my job, and I've been with the same company for over 20 years. I know I'm successful and that others count on me to come up with smart, cost-effective solutions that work, even when the challenge is difficult.

I love Johnny. As his mom, I've always loved him unconditionally, but I couldn't deal with the stress of feeling like I couldn't help him. It seemed like I'd go to bed every night fighting back tears. Some mornings before work, I'd cry in the shower so no one could hear me. I'd ask myself, 'How can I go to work and figure out how to prevent a huge bridge from falling down, but not be able to help my 6-year-old son sit in a chair?'

Accepting my perceived failure was unbearable. I had to

face the fact that I couldn't fix it. I couldn't make everything better today, and that thinking I should was stressing me to the point of breaking. I was actually less stressed when I finally admitted that I couldn't fix it. I was able to spend less energy stressing over my failures with John and more energy getting to know my son, who's a wonderful, beautiful child."

"I couldn't accept the situation until I could forgive myself."

Rita's Story:

"I recall saying that I accepted what was going on with our son, Ray. I accepted the new way of life. However, looking back, I can see I didn't grasp the implications. Ray's father accepted it more than I did. I was a wreck. I couldn't catch up. It seemed like when one problem was solved, there was another and another. Life seemed like a big math problem, weighing what was good against what was bad for this child. When people would ask me what was wrong, I wanted to scream, 'Everything!'

I remember when we bought Ray's wheelchair. We finally found one that fit him and he could roll by himself. Soon after, we discovered he had atrophy in the discs in his back and couldn't sit in a chair without a special device for spine support. The device made him feel better, but he no longer fit in the wheelchair. He needed one with more depth. I'm starting to believe that when we solve one problem, two new ones arise. I had to step back and accept that we were always going to have two, or even 10, new challenges.

While talking with my friends and family about my

frustration, I realized I was blaming myself for all the problems. With each new problem, I felt a new wave of guilt sweep over me.

I thought about what I could've done to cause my child all these problems, but I really couldn't come up with anything that made sense. I just felt that I carried him. Therefore, something about me must have gone wrong.

I finally told my husband about how guilty I felt. He couldn't believe why or how I could feel that way. He helped me work through my list of what-ifs and made it possible for me to forgive myself and accept the situation. I was able to let go of the guilt and stop reviewing everything I may have done right or wrong during my pregnancy. Once I accepted the notion of forgiving myself, I was able to relax, re-channel my blame energy and acknowledge that I wasn't the problem, nor could I solve the problem. Together, we replaced the word 'problem' with 'challenge,' 'hurdle' or 'bump in the road.'

Forgiveness allowed me to accept that I had to refocus and share what I was thinking and feeling with my husband, even if it was difficult to say or hear.

Ray is our gift. He's a beautiful, happy and caring little boy who somehow figured out how to play, laugh, learn and love all of us, even on days of unbearable pain."

My Thoughts: Forgiveness doesn't mean to forget or erase what was or what is. Choosing to forgive allows us to move forward, get past it and let go of emotional pain, bitterness and the "what if" questions. Self-forgiveness is a powerful choice that clears the path before us. Forgiveness doesn't require that we forget.

"I'm an accountant. I figure things out, follow rules and solve problems in ways that make sense."

Mark's Story:

"I'm a no-nonsense guy who thinks in a straight line. When our child was sick with cancer, I had no idea how to react or respond to the situation. It made no sense to me. In my world, I look at a problem, figure out the solution, add up numbers to make it work and that's the end of it. I thought I was in some sort of bad dream when I rushed to the hospital to be at my 3-year-old daughter's bedside. I could hardly find her in a bed surrounded by pumps, tubes and machines. She reached out her hand for me. I could hardly look.

By the third day, she woke up, held her hand out toward me and said, 'Help me, Daddy.' When she did that, I felt emotionally paralyzed. It was as if I was on the other side of the room, watching a scene from a movie. I was angry, aggravated and sick to my stomach. I couldn't make sense of it. My way of dealing with problems was never going to work in this situation. It seemed impossible. Nothing was clear. No answer was sure. Things changed daily, and time stood still. I couldn't put numbers into a calculator and get an answer. I felt like I was being forced to surrender. I wanted to blame something or someone for the cancer, but there was nowhere to put the blame. Cancer just was. I had no choice but to accept that I had to wait, listen and try to trust the doctors in charge. I struggled, but I learned I needed to take breaks from thinking and beating myself up for not coming up with a solution.

Believe it or not, my 3-year-old was my teacher. This little girl taught me how to take a 'thinking break.' She taught me how to play. When I'm with her, we talk, sing, blow bubbles, read, play, glue stuff and color. Once I accepted that I wasn't going to be the hero who hid behind my computer searching for a quick miracle, I started to accept the situation. I've accepted that treatment is a long, slow process filled with waiting, re-evaluating and hoping.

Now, when she reaches her hand to me, I reach back. I hold her hand and accept that she needs me to be there—at that moment—with her. I can't fix this today. This isn't easy math."

"I have to accept that there are no answers."

Paul's Story:

"It's been over 20 years and I'm still asking myself, 'What is the diagnosis here?' 'What went wrong?' We brought our child to hundreds of doctors, scans, tests, therapies and interventions. I finally stopped focusing on having to have an answer and started to accept that I may never know. But my heart may never fully accept this because I still can't believe it. How can I understand something I can't see? For now, I have to accept that medical science can't figure this out."

My Thoughts: Many parents and caregivers agree that it's heartbreaking to see other children develop, make friends and play sports, while your child seems stuck having to learn and re-learn tasks that seem so simple. Accepting the slower pace of learning, socializing and understanding can be difficult, especially when compared with kids the same age, who seem to sail along without a problem.

"I had to accept that my child would do normal things, but much later than normal."

Matthew's Story:

"I worried about my son Todd keeping up. As a dad, I wanted him to experience boy things like I did when I was a kid. I was frustrated when I tried to help him keep up and he couldn't. He was frustrated with me at times, and I had to learn when to back off. As time went on, the difference between Todd and kids his age grew larger and larger. I had to accept that Todd wouldn't be doing what other kids do.

He couldn't participate in typical activities like baseball or football because he couldn't understand the game. He can't really be part of a team.

One day it hit me that Todd would never get a driver's license, live on his own or go away to college. Everything was different. His social life was different and, as a result, so was ours. As a dad, I was hurt and felt sorry for Todd because he wouldn't be able to do the things that I did as a kid. Over time, I realized Todd had his own life that moved at its own unique pace. A few typical kids accepted him, his slower pace, slurred speech—his normal way of doing things. They accept that he's different. And when Todd is with them, he doesn't worry about keeping up.

Todd taught me to accept that there's a normal and a Todd normal. I love and accept the Todd normal and wouldn't change him, even if I could. He's 11 years old now. He plays sports, has friends in social clubs and loves his new cell phone. He found his group of friends who are more like him. And he laughs, learns to compete and has fun."

"I fell to the floor."

Austin's Story:

"I know the doctor was trying to help me understand what was going on, but it had been only 20 minutes. Just 20 minutes before, I got THE phone call that's every parent's worst nightmare. I remember hearing, 'Get to the hospital! Steve was walking, got hit by a train and lost both legs – but he's alive.' As I listened, my heart felt like it was about to jump out of my chest. My world stopped and my body felt like it was moving in a slow-motion panic.

I arrived at the hospital in shock. But knowing my child

was alive helped me accept the situation. I saw Steve for only five minutes before the doctor asked to speak with our family in the hallway. She began talking about all the bad stuff that could happen, including infections, blood clots, bleeding and the need for pain medications. It was too much. I just couldn't take it all in. It was too soon. As Steve's doctor continued, I fainted, crashing to the floor. I ended up being a patient for an hour or so until they knew I was OK. Later, when I walked back into Steve's room, all he could do was laugh. He said, 'Dad, don't try to get all the attention here! I need you.'

It was amazing to see a perfectly healthy, athletic kid who had just lost half his body making jokes and worrying about my well-being. He accepted the loss of his legs and realized that his being alive was more than a small miracle.

It's been over a year since I—a Marine—fainted at the hospital. The one and maybe only thing that has helped me accept the situation is Steve. My son is remarkable. He makes everyone feel at ease with his attitude, humor and motivation to walk, finish school and become an athlete again. Re-learning how to balance, walk, drive and climb stairs hasn't been easy, but he's determined and fiercely competitive. He's such a nice kid, and he makes what seems impossible look so easy. He hardly complains, and he still laughs at me for fainting. I'm so happy he's alive that I'll gladly listen to anything he has to say."

"I had to accept that I have to wait for my child to do things that take others almost no time at all."

Bob's Story:

"It's overwhelming—the waiting for Jason to get dressed, find his shoes and speak a few words. I had to get used to waiting. My father didn't wait for me to do things. He yelled a lot and would become frustrated and irritated. My father wasn't a very patient man. I had to accept that I couldn't be like him. Jason taught me how to wait, be patient and pay attention to what's going on right now. He also taught me unconditional love. I didn't even know what the word actually meant until a therapist explained it during a group meeting. I felt like she was describing Jason. Jason loves me, my wife and actually everyone. He's overly affectionate, and he can see when someone else is upset or hurt by something. It's like he has special insight. I have a long way to go, but Jason helps me face the challenge of being patient and enjoy the moment instead of hurrying to the next thing. I love my father. But I can't be like him. Now I'm a patient man who often says, 'Yep, we're late, but we're here.'"

My Thoughts: Children are born with the ability to unconditionally love. They love us on good days and on bad ones. And they love us on days when we don't even like ourselves.

"I believe God gave me this child."

Sue's Story:

"I believed from the first day I was pregnant that birth is a miracle and children are gifts from God. We knew from the start that our child had special needs and wouldn't talk or walk. He's my first child and I love him just like my other children. I accept his multiple physical and learning limitations. I didn't ask why. I didn't have to adjust to the fact that he isn't a perfectly healthy child because I didn't have expectations. I've always believed that we're all part of God's plan. And Jimmy is a part of what God has planned for me."

My Thoughts: People who know a child with special needs know they're more like than unlike other kids. Those who don't know often see the disability and not the child. We can change that.

"Life's normal, but a different kind of normal. And it isn't going to change."

JoAnn's Story:

"My husband and I get along very well now. But we didn't for the first several years because we had different expectations about how life and marriage should be. Having a child together was our dream.

We had difficulty getting pregnant, and we spent a lot of time and money trying. We expected to grow old with grandchildren and then move to Florida. We have one child named Tommy. His formal diagnosis has yet to be identified. He struggled with school, friends, sports and coordination. And he didn't always fit in with kids his age. We constantly argued about what to expect and what we should do to help

Tommy live a happy life. Once we realized that life with Tommy wasn't the normal one we'd anticipated, we began to accept that our plans had to change. We talked, laughed and cried until we finally got on the same page.

Tommy is 22 years old now, and he continues to have many special needs. He's kind, funny and considerate. And he loves his life. He has a job and friends who care about him. We made it through by adapting to Tommy's changing needs. Together, we listened to what Tommy was telling and showing us, and we figured out how to fit into his world. We learned to redefine our plans and accept the new plan that Tommy so eloquently demonstrates. We stayed here in Michigan. Our life is here. We can't move and start over. Our dream child has brought us together as a strong couple and family. And we have more happiness than we ever dreamed."

My Thoughts: Things some people take for granted are things someone else may be praying for.

"My child's world is about sameness."

Terry's Story:

"My child has been diagnosed with autism. When he was about 12 years old, I wanted him to start experiencing different things such as museums, plays and restaurants. No matter how much I tried, he wanted no part of it. I learned to accept that he felt comfortable doing his favorite things, the things he wanted to do. He'd get anxious when he was encouraged to experience something different or new. I had to back off and let him do his own thing, even if it was focused on dinosaurs, a topic with which he's familiar and comfortable. I've accepted that, once in a while, he'll try new things. And when he does, it's wonderful."

My Thoughts: Unconditionally accepting and loving our children with special needs doesn't mean accepting their situations "as is." We can advocate and lead the way to improving their quality of life for as long as it takes.

"I don't think I'm there yet. I haven't totally accepted this situation. I have in my head, but not in my heart."

Michael's story:

"I don't know marriage or home life without the demands of special needs. I'm overwhelmed with caring for a child I love who can't express his love for me. I know my life is more difficult than those who don't have this challenge. It's extremely difficult and time consuming. I'm not there yet, but I've learned to accept that I need to talk to others, especially other fathers like me, and ask them to help me deal with this. Just listening to myself answer this question is helpful."

"I'm ashamed to say I'm angry with God. I
love my son more than anything, but accepting
this is hard because I think it's unfair."

Tina's Story:

"I have only one child, and I love him. I was angry with God for a long time because I could have only one child. We did everything to have another, but we just couldn't. I don't understand a God who would do this. A child with special needs should never be the first child—and never the only child. I'm still trying to accept this. I may one day."

"I had to accept that I was in a real depression."

Emma's Story:

"Somehow I made it through. But at first, I couldn't believe my daughter, Carrie, was born with Down syndrome. I felt so bad for her, for us, and I was in a constant state of fear. This was a total surprise to us, and I couldn't accept it at first. I didn't realize it, but I was extremely depressed. I had to leave work, and I couldn't sleep or eat for about three or four days. My mom had to move in with us. I tried to nurse Carrie, but she wouldn't latch on. Some days I just sat on the couch and rocked back and forth. My friends and family were worried about how depressed I had become. I didn't realize how bad I was.

Before Carrie was born, I worked full time as a nurse. I was organized and had family parties all the time. Now, I was in some kind of deep hole. I was unable to shower, have a conversation or enjoy anything. I had to accept that depression had taken over me, and I had to deal with it. I had to talk about it and not hide within myself. I accepted the help I needed in order to deal with fear and to find myself again. I was worried that other people would think I didn't want Carrie because she was diagnosed with Down syndrome.

It wasn't that. It was the shock and fear about the diagnosis I couldn't handle. Getting help for depression helped me to deal with all my guilt. I felt like a terrible mom, wife and daughter for not taking care of my baby and for worrying my family so much. Carrie is our beautiful little girl. I'm reminded of how blessed I am each time she calls me Mom."

My Thoughts: Feeling overwhelming fear and stress can cause depression, isolation and the inability to function as your usual self. It's not just you. A lot of people find themselves in the deep hole of depression. Get help.

My Thoughts: Deal with fear instead of giving it control. Build a reserve of perseverance and courage.

1 **Acceptance** *A Look Back*

Anyone's child can be born with or develop some type of medical or mental health condition. Anyone's child can be involved in an accident, resulting in life-altering challenges. The color of your skin, level of your education, size of your bank account or your religious beliefs won't make a difference. Disabilities don't discriminate.

The majority of parents and caregivers agree that accepting that life has changed—but goes on—is the first step toward achieving a *New Normal*. It's much more than a mindset. It's a balance of challenges, achievements, sorrows and joys that makes life rewarding for your child, your family and you.

"Over the years, my students have taught me that every child can learn. I keep each child's uniqueness and individual learning style in mind as I teach my students new skills, reinforce skills they have learned and celebrate their accomplishments. They teach me as I teach them."
—*Kim Taylor, Special Education Teacher, Brecksville/Broadview Heights Middle School*

2 Learning About You

I MAGINE INTERACTING WITH THE PEOPLE around you, but doing so with one or more extra challenges. Imagine not having the ability to drive, speak, hear, see or understand the underlying meaning of a situation. Despite having one or more of these limitations, your attitude is positive and you're pleasant, kind and smart.

Unfortunately, at school, at work and in the neighborhood, some people avoid you, asssuming you're unable to function like everybody else. Intimidated by what they don't understand, these people don't initiate talking or interacting with you in any way. It's difficult to observe others who are hesitant or even fearful about welcoming you into their social groups because, in their minds, you're a BIG question mark.

This metaphorical question mark represents a mystery label that some people place on others who are different. Not necessarily bad, just different.

Despite all these challenges, our children are happy, patient with others and willing to try new things. Most of all, they are forgiving.

They forgive those around them who can be negative, insensitive or even unpleasant. Amazingly and endearingly, our kids are willing to give others another chance. In fact, our children remain hopeful that, this time, the people who didn't inititally accept them will try to get to know them and ultimately want to be their friend.

When I asked parents to share a special or surprising moment along their journey, many gave this response: "When I began to see the world from my child's perspective."

These parents went on to say that what surprised them the most was not what they learned about their children— but rather what they discovered about themselves.

For real-life examples, read on.

"I learned to put my hopefulness in perspective and not believe everything I read."

Mary's Story:

"Once I understood the nature of my daughter's diagnosis, I started reading anything and everything I could. The list was endless: her condition, medications, assessments, case studies, doctor profiles and places that could possibly help. I was excited each time I read about a successful intervention or treatment. And I put all my energy into finding out how to access the medications, doctors, articles or cures identified. I knew I was doing a good thing by educating myself. However, I didn't realize how my emotions were affected by what I was reading or by what others would suggest I do. I had to learn to be an objective reader, not an emotional one. Before I learned how to do this, my emotions would go up and down all day. In an hour, I'd go from excitement and hopeful joy to feeling like someone had just punched me in the stomach. I could hardly see past my tears.

However, once I learned to be objective, I stopped the emotional ups and downs, ending the constant cycle of excitement and defeat. I was able to selectively ask questions and not freak out at the first sign of adversity. Good or bad news, not everything I read was true. I'm still learning, still feeling the ups and downs. But now I can put my hopefulness in perspective with confidence and be the expert my child needs."

My Thoughts: Someone else's idea of what you should do isn't always what YOU should do.

"I learned I couldn't ignore God and my spiritual side."

Jim's Story:

"I'm not a religious person and neither is my family. I didn't grow up knowing God, church or prayer. In fact, I used to ignore the entire topic of religion. Now, it's in my face and I can't ignore it. I keep asking why God thought I could handle a child with so many problems and needs. I learned I could handle the stress. But I wonder why he gave me this child when I could be doing other things to reach out to more people. I have no idea when I started to really believe that there is a God, but I do. I feel some type of inner strength to deal with this situation and handle the emotions, stress and fear of it all. I never saw my own dad's fear. I don't think my three kids can say that about me. They see my fear about our situation, but they also see my strength. I believe it's my spiritual strength. I'm more calm and at peace on difficult days and more grateful on good days. I found strength in prayer, and I continue to ask God to help me be a better man and father. And I believe I am."

"I came to realize the up-and-down waves would never end."

Rebecca's Story:

"I have four children. Three of my children are typical and one has special needs. Like with any family, parenting and taking care of four children has its ups and downs. However, with Kayla, the ups and downs are hundreds of feet higher— and hundreds of feet lower. And they're ever changing. I wish I would've known the waves would never end. I was always hopeful that things would settle down and we could have a life that was more even-keeled rather than so often in crisis mode. In time, I realized that the up-and-down waves were not going to stop and my daily routine probably wouldn't be smooth. With that realization, though, I found my strength. I learned that I'll be knocked down many times, but I have the strength to get up as many times as I fall. I found my strength in my spiritual side, prayer and my faith. I can't believe how strong of a person I've become. I can cope, and I find that my other children are stronger and more caring than they probably would be had we not had Kayla."

"I learned to pace myself."

Chantel's Story:

"I wish I'd known how long this was going to last, so I could've paced myself better in the beginning. I'm so thankful for girlfriends. They helped me learn how to take one step at a time. I learned to manage my time and my schedule. My friends remind me that I don't have to get everything done on my to-do list. One time they surprised me by coming over with their kids, who stayed and watched my son, Neil, while my friends and I went out to dinner. My girlfriends did my makeup and hair. I had fun, and I realized I'd forgotten what fun felt like. Pacing my energy so I can keep a balance has been my lifesaver."

My Thoughts: Resilience is a character strength that often results in success. But it can lead to exhaustion if our goals are unrealistic and our expectations impossibly high. Pace your energy and keep today's goals realistic.

"I learned this isn't the end of the world
and that I can handle fear."

Jill's Story:

"I had a terrible pregnancy after learning from the ultrasound that something was wrong and my child was going to have special needs. I wish I'd known that my level of fear was unnecessary. My fears screamed constantly in my head throughout the pregnancy. 'Oh my God! We're going to have this burden, this terrible interruption of life and the fear of the unknown.' I couldn't get past the fact that babies are supposed to make you happy, fill you with joy and improve your life. I wish it didn't take me so long to realize that I could take control of the fear if I took a step back. I'd constantly cry to my mom, who convinced me to go talk with someone.

Finally, I went to talk with a psychologist. I talked, cried and learned that I can handle fear. My mom went with me a few times, and she was just as worried as I was. My child is 6 years old now. And although she has learning and speech problems, she can learn, play and enjoy kindergarten like the other kids, despite needing help like using an iPad to communicate. My child's disability wasn't the end of the world. It was the beginning of a new world I knew nothing about. I love my life, and she's the most joyful part of it."

My Thoughts: Grandparents often have "double grief." They worry not only about their grandchild struggling with medical and developmental challenges, but also about their adult child's well-being. Keeping grandparents involved may help them understand how best to support the entire family.

"I learned that I could work through it."

Eric's Story:

"I wish I'd known that no matter what I ended up facing,

I'd be able to work through it. I remember the many times I wished for a normal life, because I didn't want to face this or deal with it. I learned to face one issue at a time. If I'd known this was going to last a lifetime and I'd always have to deal with problem after problem, I think I would've considered quitting. But since quitting was never a real option, I learned to believe in myself. As a result, I came to realize I was a stronger person than I could've ever imagined. People say to me, 'Wow! You're such a good dad.' I've learned to smile and say, 'Thank you.' But I know, in the beginning, I was torn apart. I was weak and sort of a coward. I'm ashamed of myself for that. But as time went on, I followed my son Jimmy's lead. He doesn't think about quitting. He gets up and smiles—even on the most difficult days. The kid is amazing. If he can do it, I can too."

"I learned to take a breath and not freak out."

Greg's Story:

"I wish I knew how important it was not to freak out. I had to learn to control my emotions. I learned that freaking out was what I do when I'm stressed. I wish I'd realized in the beginning that this isn't a good use of my energy and that I'd need energy to solve big problems. So I learned to pick my battles carefully and prioritize my energy."

My Thoughts: Figuring out the first step isn't always quick or easy. For many, the first step is finding the strength to handle fear, manage time and deal with the fact that you may always have less control than you'd like.

"I wished I learned early on to take the paperwork home."

Carol's Story:

"I must have filled out a thousand forms by the time my son was 5 years old. I wish I would have asked to take the papers home. I wouldn't have felt rushed to complete them at the doctor's office or at my son's school. I would have had more time to communicate with medical and school staff members. Instead, I was trying to remember things as I filled out form after form. Eventually, I learned to take the papers home and spend my time asking questions and actually talking with the staff."

"I realized that I could figure it out."

Rachael's Story:

"I learned I can love someone so deeply that when they hurt, I can figure it out, even though my child has no way of telling me. I learned to ask questions and not care if it's a 'stupid' one. When I was a kid, I was hesitant to raise my hand in school. Now, I can ask anything, anywhere and to anyone. I learned to tell myself, 'If I think it, I can ask it.'"

"I learned to be tenacious."

Tina's Story:

"I knew nothing about the medical or educational system and how it worked. But I came to realize that I'm relentless and tenacious. And I won't entertain the option of being passive or giving up. I learned how to navigate financial, medical, educational and political systems to find resources for my child. I learned to find the special resources available for my special child. I also realized that I'm strong, and I won't give up until I find what we need. If you keep looking, the answers and options are there. I help other moms and dads find their way through the red tape. Seeing their children thrive is the best feeling ever."

My Thoughts: No situation or person can take away your determination, intuition, passion, attitude or knowledge gained through struggles and triumphs. They are yours. The strength you need is within you. It's not the challenge that weakens us. It's the way we handle it that makes the difference.

"I realized that I isolated myself from others."

Jennifer's Story:

"I used to complain that other people stayed away from me and my child because of her special needs. But I was wrong. I was the one who gradually isolated myself from family and friends after having a child who couldn't keep up with other children his age. I stopped calling friends, visiting family and going out to movies, plays and dinners. I gradually distanced myself from friends who had typically developing children. Staying away from others was my way of denial and avoiding the reality of having a child with special needs. Gradually, I isolated from everyone. My brother helped me realize that it was me, not them. After realizing this, I made a choice to do something about it. I learned that it was *me* who determined my level of isolation.

"The only way to fail is to quit."

Kevin's Story:

"I learned to redefine failure. Failure isn't doing the wrong thing, getting the wrong answer or getting no answer at all. Failure is when you quit. When I was young, I quit many things like high school football, college and many jobs. Having Emma taught me that I no longer have that option. My only option is to listen, love my child and figure it out. I wish I'd realized I had the strength not to quit a long time ago. Emma taught me this. You should see how she learns things. I can't believe it. She tries and tries so hard, and she never quits."

"I learned how to listen."

Jerry's Story:

"I always thought I was a good listener. I've been married twice and both my ex-wife and new wife say I don't listen well. Of course I ignored their comments. Then we had Joey. Joey taught me to listen. He speaks slowly and doesn't always say what he wants to the first time or even the second. So I have to be patient, listen to each word and then help him put it all together. It may sound stupid, but it wasn't until I was 45 years old that *I* finally realized it's impossible to listen when you're talking. Now, I take a deep breath and listen to what I hear rather than think about what I want to say. Joey taught me how to do this, and I'm getting to know him more each day. I finally get it. This little boy is the best teacher for this old man."

"I learned that I'm stronger than I think
and that I can make a difference."

Carrie's Story:

"I'm a quiet, passive person. I usually listen to what's being said. I was quiet at school, and I'm the quiet one at work. I never thought I had it in me to be the leader of a conversation. I never thought I'd be the one asking the questions and being the least passive person at the table. I learned to be assertive. Now I write things down, prepare notes for school meetings and doctor appointments, and make myself heard. I'm most comfortable in the background. But when it comes to Emily, I practice and even force myself to speak up despite being nervous. Emily doesn't know this about me. She's only 6. However, it's funny and ironic that when she's with me at the doctor's office or school meetings, she claps and laughs when I start to talk and read from my notes. We all just smile."

"I learned I can love someone that much."

Kaitlyn's Story:

"I learned that I'm pretty tough—tougher than I thought. I can be assertive like I've never been before. I learned that I have to be the advocate for my child. I'm his voice when he literally doesn't have one. I look back and know I could've been stronger early on. I used to follow the suggestions of doctors and nurses without questioning their opinions, even when my gut feeling was telling me differently. I did that in the beginning because I was scared and unsure. I felt like I was in some sort of dream or nightmare. My son is 21 years old now. Over the years, I've learned to ask questions and assert myself. My son still needs me, and I can be totally selfless. I learned that I could love someone that much and give so much more than I ever thought I could."

My Thoughts: Listening to the perceptions, experiences, knowledge and opinions of others can be helpful. However, you know your child best. Your intuition cannot be exchanged or replaced by what others say.

"I'm learning to say, 'Yes, I need help.'"

Lou's Story:

"I was in the Army for half my life. I like helping others, but I almost never ask anyone for help. I've always been able to do anything I needed to do and just deal with situations as they come. But once I got the call that my teenage son was in a terrible accident, I changed. Of course I stayed at the hospital for weeks. And I drove him to therapy and follow-up appointments to help him adjust to life in a wheelchair. I'll do anything for him. However, I couldn't do anything for me. I couldn't do even simple, mundane things. I knew I had to take a shower, eat, answer the phone and talk to my family and friends. But I just couldn't.

I look back now and see that once my son was able to live his life, although now different, I was the one who needed help. It was an eye-opener when my 17-year-old son told me he didn't want help, either. But he had to accept it after the accident. He said, 'Dad, you are more paralyzed than me. Let them do stuff for you so you can get it together.' After that, I still can't say the words 'I need help.' But I say yes to those who offer. It was humbling to hear my son's words of wisdom."

My Thoughts: Try not to ignore the people you know well and who care. At times, we avoid burdening others with our fears and challenges because we believe others may not relate. The pressure of keeping thoughts and feelings to yourself can create additional stress. Instead, try to allow those who love you to help.

"I learned that I don't have to explain myself."

Halle's Story:

"I was the type of person who felt like I owed others an explanation about what's going on. This was especially true whenever others would stare at us in a store or at a school function or sporting event. When I noticed a stranger staring as I tried to calm Alec down, I'd automatically turn to that person and volunteer information about our situation. It happened a lot. When Alec was between 3 and 10 years old, he had many special needs, and I was simply exhausted. He didn't sleep. I didn't sleep. He couldn't speak clearly, and he was unbalanced because of cerebral palsy. When he was frustrated, he'd scream in stores, at playgrounds – anywhere. It took all day to do one thing, and I felt bad for him because he couldn't shake the frustration. In some ways, I wanted to explain to the whole world how difficult life was for Alec. If I did, would they understand—or even care?

Finally, I realized that I didn't have to. I learned to manage the anxiety I had about being judged. I actually felt like I was being punished—not by Alec—but by the stares, glares and eye rolls of others. I learned to ignore it all and focus my energy on Alec and how I could alleviate my frustration. I don't have to explain myself to anyone. Others may see me as an aloof, air-headed or arrogant person one day and a warm, smart, loving parent the next. Who cares? I know who I am, and it's beyond my control what others may think at that moment."

"I learned to change my expectations."

Tim's Story:

"Almost everyone in my family went to college. Most of us are successful. When my wife and I had children, we started saving for college before our kids could crawl. I never imagined having a child who couldn't read or write. Alex was born with a small brain tumor. It was surgically removed several times, but it always grew back. By the age of six, Alex had a lot of the right side of his brain removed and parts of the left. I was shocked to hear that our treatment options were narrowing and that brain-tissue removal became our best option. Alex was happy, kind and all the other good things every parent wants his or her child to be. But college was always out of the question. Alex made me accept that he wasn't able to do or learn some things I had dreamed for him. I learned to change my expectations and focus on what he could do.

That lesson, as well as many other life lessons Alex so gracefully demonstrated, stayed with me, even after his death. I go on with his courage, strength and smile in my heart."

My Thoughts: Life from the perspective of children with special needs isn't always familiar or common. What may be a small hurt to others may a big hurt to them. And what looks like a small accomplishment to others may be a big accomplishment through the eyes of these children. Learn to celebrate and respond accordingly.

"I learned financial planning."

Robert's Story:

"I'm used to being the guy who helps others, and I'm very open to friends and family who call me up to lend an ear or give advice. As my child grew up, I realized that he needed long-term financial planning to cover the many expenses he could not afford by himself. I was confused, at first, because financial planning for a child with special needs isn't the same as it is for our other children. I learned about it. I educated myself on rules about taxes, government benefits, maximum savings accounts, planning a will and guardianship for my son. It was an eye-opener for me. And asking for help, admitting once again I'm powerless in this situation, was difficult."

My Thoughts: In a perfect world, we would live forever. Start early and consult experts who know how to plan for the financial future of a child who may not live or work independently.

"I learned to put my 'big girl' panties on."

Bethany's Story:

"I had a way of avoiding family and friends. I'm not sure how I got into the habit of avoiding because this is not typical of me. One day, while talking with a neighbor, I figured it out. It was all about my fear. I was afraid that people who knew me well would find out how miserable I was with myself. I was miserable because I didn't believe I could handle the responsibility of tending to the needs of my daughter, Sarah, day in and day out. Sometimes I hated it and just wanted to scream. I kept saying to myself, 'How heartless am I?' It isn't Sarah's fault she needs medications and surgeries to repair the damage caused by some type of cardiovascular disease.' I was avoiding others because I was afraid. I was afraid to be judged for not believing I could do this, for not wanting to be here and for being such a weak person and mom. Eventually, I stopped hiding because the pain of being lonely was just as bad as the fear of being judged. I started talking about it. My life became real again. And I realized that my family and friends listened and were not as judgmental as I had feared. Once I learned to put my 'big girl' panties on and stop hiding, I felt a sense of relief."

"I learned the meaning of passion."

Val's Story:

"I learned that my passion for Joey's needs has no limits."

My Thoughts: Sometimes it's best to take action and change the direction of how things are going. Other times, it's best to go with the flow. Figure out if what's in front of you is a stepping-stone or a stumbling block. Then decide what to do.

2 Learning About You *A Look Back*

All around the world, parents and caregivers of children with special needs have discovered strengths they never knew they had. By rising to the challenges placed before them, they've grown as parents, partners and individuals in ways they couldn't have imagined. Those interviewed agree that although we learn at our own pace, we eventually learn what to do, how to cope and how to determine what our children need by listening to them. Our children teach us to see life from their perspective. They inspire us to focus on what's important, from their vantage point. We can step back from our fears to objectively educate ourselves, enabling us to become strong advocates for our children. We can accept that we're not alone and that putting our faith in a higher power or accepting help from others is not a weakness.

"When my son walked out of the house wearing his hearing implants for the first time, I saw him stop and look up at a tree. He had just heard a bird. I cried tears of joy because I realized that I had just seen him hear for the first time. I can't say that about my other kids, but I can with this child. Watching my son hear was one of the best experiences I have ever had. It was a miracle."

—*Deanna O'Donnell, JD,*
Parma Municipal Court Judge

3 Understanding What Your Child Can and Can't Do—Yet

MANY PEOPLE ARE SENSITIVE ABOUT the heartbreak. It's sometimes shocking to discover that a child's physical, medical or emotional challenge may interfere with his or her development and learning. Although it's inspiring to celebrate the many things our children can do, the harsh reality of what they can't accomplish is heard loud and clear.

Parents and caregivers were asked, "Of the experiences you've had, what stands out the most as you look back on your journey?"

There were many responses. But one of the most intriguing replies reflected hope. "Watching my child try—without success—to complete a task would inspire my sense of hope. Also, I was reminded of skills and activities typical kids their age seem to learn and master so automatically or quickly."

These parents and caregivers went on to explain that as disappointed and defeated as they felt at the time, they later discovered that these seemingly impossible activities were actually quite doable—in time.

Let's put the "can't do" message into perspective. There are things most children will accomplish, and there are things most children won't accomplish. And this reality will hold true throughout their adult lives. For example, most children will not grow up to be pilots, professional athletes, CEOs of companies or the president of the United States.

In this way, our children are just like everyone else. Regardless of our hopes and dreams, most parents and caregivers of children with special needs realize that what our children can achieve is impossible to predict. Sometimes our children have difficulty learning skills we expected they would learn easily. Other times, they develop skills beyond all expectations.

Either way, the pride, joys and happiness we get from our children by watching their determination, tenacity and successes in life, despite the odds being stacked against them, can be amazing. There is a wealth of stories about how children with special needs amaze their parents, caregivers and friends with their skills, knowledge, insight and kindness toward others.

"Seth is sensitive and compassionate."

Jody's Story:

"Seth didn't even talk until he was 7 years old. He's 17

years old now, and we still don't have a label or diagnosis that explains all his delays. He can't speak with perfect clarity, but he can speak so that others understand him. For a child who couldn't say a word for years, I'm always amazed at how compassionate and sensitive he is toward others. He asks everyone, 'How are you?' And he really wants to know. He listens and is patient with others. He remembers things about other people and expresses genuine concern. Once my neighbor had a bad cold. When we saw her a few months later, Seth remembered and asked her how she was and if she was still taking medicine. Even she forgot about her cold, but not Seth. He remembered and cared enough to ask."

*"Sarah can think for herself and come
up with creative solutions."*

Don's Story:

"My daughter Sarah can't speak. She can't utter a sound. She uses a soundboard to spell out the words and then the machine talks for her. The voice on the machine sounds strange, but it works and she can communicate. Before we had her, I connected one's ability to talk with one's ability to think. I was so wrong. Now I understand it differently. Even though Sarah has never spoken a word, she is creative and can think out problems, generating options and solutions. She can think for herself, argue and disagree with you and even explain her view logically. I know many people without special needs who can't problem solve or discuss topics like that. She's good at communicating and very proud. Her only limitation is the patience of others."

My Thoughts: Success requires taking risks, dealing with ups and downs and failing at parts of a task. We can fail, succeed or not try at all. The worst option is not to try because it eliminates all possibilities.

"She's simply hilarious."

My Story:

"She has a sense of humor that amazes me. She understands what jokes and comments are appropriate for adults and what's appropriate for kids. Although she speaks with a stutter, she knows exactly what she wants to say. Her words seem to get stuck at times, and when she tries to say what is on her mind, some people lose patience. They don't wait to listen to her finish a sentence, or they finish the sentence for her, which is so frustrating. However, when she's talking with a group of people who listen to her jokes and funny comments, she has the whole room laughing. Her smile is contagious. She makes people laugh at home, school, during a game – everywhere. She's just fun. Sometime's it's hard to believe that a child who has suffered so much could be so pleasant and happy. Love her."

"She hasn't learned that not everyone can be trusted."

Chuck's Story:

"She hasn't learned that some people aren't nice and

shouldn't be trusted. Kids and adults have hurt her in the past and yet she still doesn't approach new people with caution. Thinking that kids like her and want to be her friend, she's been teased and asked to do silly things. They're actually making fun of her, but she doesn't realize it. Others have stolen her money, watches and food. We continue to talk with her about this and point out the bad things that have happened. We constantly tell her that she needs to be careful and not assume others can be trusted. She understands what we're saying, but she doesn't seem to connect one example to the next. She continues to believe that if someone is nice, they can be trusted."

"He can't defend himself."

Bob's Story:

"I had to come to the realization that he can't defend himself, and I'm not sure that other people would watch out for him. He's a vulnerable target for others who are reckless and careless.

It got even tougher when I gave him a cell phone. I wanted him to have one so we could reach each other easily. Unfortunately, other kids have persuaded him to prank call others, use swear words and take pictures of others without their knowledge. I look through his phone, and I can't believe some of the language these kids are using, even some of the 'good' kids.

I had hoped by the time he was a teenager, he could understand who he can and he can't trust. I don't think he could get himself out of a bad situation, so I make sure he's with someone who will take care of him and protect him. In the past year, he's been better at thinking through situations and understanding when he needs to say no. But we aren't there yet."

"He can talk."

Patricia's Story:

"He has speech. I describe it as developing in slow motion. I really didn't think he'd ever be able to talk, but he can. He started with one vowel sound, and then one consonant sound, followed by one word, then two. By the age of eight or nine, he finally started putting sentences together. He's 16 years old now and can talk. He can speak in sentences, but he can't talk in a social situation and make friends. I'm not saying he couldn't do that some day. But for now, it's a huge challenge for him to talk with kids his age, much less have a meaningful conversation like friends do. He socializes with kids his age by participating with them in a sport or riding his bike alongside them. Some of his cousins and friends at school understand his speech, and it's wonderful to watch them listen to him. The teachers at school encourage him and they're my angels."

My Thoughts: Include your child in everything you can, from family vacations, parties and celebrations to decisions, activities and functions.

"He can throw a ball, dribble a ball and walk the dog."

Ellen's Story:

"His physical abilities are amazing, considering where we started."

"I thought she'd be better socially."

Linda's Story:

"I really thought my daughter would be able to socialize with her peers when she became a teenager. However, she hasn't matured. She has mood swings and anxiety that make it difficult for her to initiate friendships. She'd rather be alone most of the time. Kids her age notice quickly that she's confused, nervous and not a 'natural' in the group. I feel unprepared to help her interact socially with friends. She does well academically, but socializing is another story. Staying on the topic of the conversation and looking at the person who's talking are skills she just can't seem to learn quickly. Maybe in time."

"I never thought that, at age 17, eating would be a problem."

Michelle's Story:

"Eric hasn't learned to eat properly. He shoves food into his mouth so fast that we've had to perform the Heimlich maneuver on him. Eric can't feel the food in his mouth, so he puts too much food in at a time. He doesn't have the jaw strength to chew his food, so he chokes. Eating is a skill that usually comes naturally, but not for him. It interferes with his social, family and school life several times a day. I try not to worry about it when he's away from me, like when he's at school. But it's a challenge *not* to worry about him. I worry that Eric will choke, but more so, I worry about how embarrassed he may feel if he ever notices people are staring at him when he does this."

"Kyle can't run fast, but he can play basketball."

Ray's Story:

"Kyle seemed to be a perfectly healthy baby. But when he was 18 months old, he had a seizure in his crib. Within minutes, we were rushing him to the hospital. His brain was swelling, and it was determined that he'd had a stroke.

Although Kyle had immediate medical care, his walking and talking were delayed, and he has many physical challenges. He may never be able to hold himself upright. And he may always walk with a limp, having to drag his left leg. Although Kyle has almost no use of his left arm, at age 5 he started playing basketball with me out in the driveway. I played on my college basketball team and love the game.

Kyle is 11 years old now. With only one arm, he can dribble and make baskets. I still can't believe how fast he can dribble and control the ball down the court. He's a bit slower than other kids and he'll never make a high school basketball team. But he can play pick-up games with kids his age."

My Thoughts: We repeat steps over and over to help our children learn what other's may learn easily, if not automatically. Once our children get it, we celebrate because, once again, our children have given us another chance to witness a miracle.

"Larry still isn't accepted by other kids."

Roger's Story:

"Larry is just not social. We try to teach him what to do in terms of saying hello, using manners, asking questions and answering them. But he just won't. I really thought more kids would've accepted him by now, but they seem to ignore him like he ignores them. It breaks my heart. However, once we shared our concern with family and some friends, they started talking to Larry and including him. All it took was saying something. I still wait for my brother to come around, and he may never. Now Larry has his group. It's actually my group of adult friends, but he fits in because they make the effort to fit him in. And as little social interaction as Larry has, he interacts, smiles and enjoys spending time with others. He's the most popular one in the group. It's so nice."

My Thoughts: Not everyone you thought would support you will. Some people just can't do it. Sometimes the people you thought would call or stick around don't. For each person who leaves, there are others who stay and appreciate what is. Be grateful for the space the others left open. You now have more room in your life for people who care and want to support you as your child grows.

"If we started therapy earlier, maybe he'd be better."

Renee's Story:

"I had a feeling something was wrong, but I was encouraged to wait and see. I wish I hadn't waited. I would've given my son more intensive therapy early on. After we finally started therapy and learning about his condition, I began to understand some of his behaviors and why he was not talking and interacting with us early on. Now I know that the earlier you can provide therapy, intervention, accommodations and treatment, the healthier your child will be. I know he can think about what he wants to say, but he still has difficulty saying it. I wonder if he would've been better if we had started speech therapy earlier. We'll never know."

My Thoughts: There's no secret book of instructions. What to do now and what to do next are sometimes guesses based on logic, experience or another new suggestion that seems to make sense.

"I thought he'd be job-ready by now."

Laura's Story:

"I thought by now, at age 18, he'd be job-ready. But he's not. Now that Mitch is almost out of school, I need to help him learn skills so he can work somewhere. I was hoping he'd learn job skills, but his nerves get in the way. He doesn't know how to react to new people, how to approach a new task or be in a new environment without pacing because he's nervous. My next 'Mom' job is to help him learn how to behave on the job. Maybe in the next few years, he'll be ready to work somewhere."

3 Understanding What Your Child Can and Can't Do–Yet *A Look Back*

Many skills that may seem impossible for your child to learn at first are likely to be ones he or she will master in time. We're our child's first teachers. We're the first to watch our children develop, and we notice when a specific skill isn't developing. Sometimes we notice this right away because our children aren't reaching early milestones. Other times, our children are developing just fine, but then seem to stop and not develop in a particular area. Regardless, most parents respond with concern. What parents and caregivers would share with those new to this situation is that what your child can't do today simply may be what he or she just can't do yet.

Of the hundreds of stories shared, the message repeated over and over again is: *Anything's possible*. It may take years of determination and practice, but many can't-do skills are actually can't-do-yet skills. Again and again, our children with special needs demonstrate that they're valuable role models for having managed physical challenges and other adversities with hope and success.

"Children with special needs are more *like*
typical children than they are not like them."
—*Sandra Delaportis, MD, Internist, Cleveland Clinic*

4 Feeling Alone

MANY PARENTS AND CAREGIVERS FEEL alone when trying to care for and understand how they can best help their children. Some parents believe that no one understands what their lives are like; others feel alone in their search for answers. We all ask "what if" questions.

What if my child were healthy?

What if my child could make friends?

What if she had strength, coordination and balance like other kids?

It's almost impossible not to wonder, but agonizing over the inability to answer impossible questions isn't a healthy way to spend the day.

Many parents and caregivers have found ways to work through feeling alone. The energy generated by the frustration often motivates parents and caregivers to reach out and take action. They share their stories so others may follow their lead.

"I feel alone when I can't get answers."

Bob's Story:

"I felt alone and frustrated the moment I realized I had no idea what to do when Emily, my 2-year-old, became ill. I'm a big guy: 6-foot-2, 265 pounds. I'm an engineer. And when I don't know something, I figure it out. I have three older kids. If I had a nickel for every time they asked me a question and I told them to look it up, I'd be a rich man.

Emily changed everything. My black-and-white thinking didn't work in this situation. In fact, it pushed me away from everyone until I was on my own island. I wanted to be the leader, protector and father like my dad. However, I felt like I was the opposite, and I didn't talk to anyone. Instead, I stayed to myself, searching for answers in books, on the Internet, in research studies, determined to heal my little girl. I wanted to put an end to the tubes, needles, monitors and complicated medical problems. The helpless feeling made me realize I was alone, and it made me sick.

I had to admit that I was miserable and not going to figure this out by myself. So I started to listen, control my anger and talk. Once I did, I still felt helpless. But I was more prepared to have a conversation with my wife and kids. I wish I had realized earlier that my black-and-white thinking wasn't helpful and my trying to find the answers on my own was a poor excuse to isolate myself. Over the years, Emily has taught me to be a listener and to be more available to my family. She has also taught me to see beyond the medical equipment. I now see Emily. The more I get to know her, the more I learn to pay attention to what's important. She was born knowing how to do that."

*"I feel most alone and confused when
dealing with the school system."*

Rita's Story:

"Eventually, I was able to turn my 'all alone' feelings into a sense of empowerment. I wish I would have understood the school system before I found myself in the middle of 504 plans, Individualized Educational Plans (IEPs) and the assessment process that involves many professionals. I heard words like 'educational goals,' 'academic accommodations,' 'criteria' and 'measurable goals.' I had no idea what all those words meant or what the school could provide.

If I could do it all over again, I'd go to meetings and seminars before my child was school-aged to learn the language, process and opportunities of special needs education. And I'd find other parents who were familiar with the school system and learn from them. I was lost in the beginning. Asking questions and keeping notes saved me from total confusion."

*"I feel alone and overwhelmed when
one problem piles on another."*

Sylvia's Story:

"I feel alone when I learn a new truth about my child's condition. I already knew it was challenging, unique and confusing—and a lot to deal with for one person. I feel very alone when I'm told that there's another problem to deal with on top of the problems we already know about. 'They found another problem?' 'This child has to go through more tests?' 'We have to change medications again?' 'We have to spend more days at the hospital?' I feel alone in a world of billions of people, thinking not one of them could truly understand this."

"I feel alone when I let the what-ifs make me feel helpless."

Lenard's Story:

"I feel alone when I realize there's no quick-fix, no solutions and no end to my child's suffering. 'What if Chad could hear or speak without a voice box and pointer pad?' Regardless of how much I wonder or hope, it isn't going to happen. And yet Chad is happy and he can express what he's thinking. He makes perfect sense and he can even win arguments. I used to make myself sick to my stomach, thinking and thinking. Chad doesn't ask, 'What if?' But I do. Over the years, I continued to let myself ask, 'What if?' But I don't let myself dwell on the question. The question is real, but pondering it isn't a good use of my time."

"Receiving get-well cards makes me wonder."

Tylena's Story:

"Cards and well wishes get me thinking, 'What if my child was healthy?' 'What if he could go outside and play like other 11-year-old kids?' I feel alone when I pray sometimes. I pray for a cure and for healing. Over the years, I've opened hundreds of cards for my child and almost every one says, 'You and your family are in our prayers. May God bless you.' Sometimes I whisper, 'God who?'"

My Thoughts: Showing your emotions lets others know how you feel. Not every day is a feel-good story filled with feel-good emotions. If they ask, tell it like it is. They'll witness your strength.

"What if my son could get married and start a family?"

Olivia's Story:

"I feel alone and very sad when my son asks me if he could find a girl, get married and have children. What if he really could? I'd have grandchildren. And he'd live independently, able to take care of himself and possibly me one day.

But I know better. He does inappropriate things like asking girls if he can kiss them—or marry them. He's friendly and always smiling, and the few girls he talks with are friendly and kind. But none of them wants to be his girlfriend. He doesn't understand relationships like marriage, and he needs help taking care of himself. He needs to be reminded to bathe, shave, get a haircut and change his clothes. He can do all these things and he's a handsome teenager. But he isn't independent. He's a sweetheart, though. When I start my 'what if' thinking, I feel left out of the group of moms with fewer challenges."

"The fear of 'what if' makes me feel alone."

Henri's Story:

"I feel very alone in my fears. I don't know which fears

are real and which ones are just in my head. I ask myself, 'What if we can't afford this?' 'What if his condition gets worse and I can't take care of him?' When I let my mind get caught up in all the what-ifs, I'm miserable."

"I feel caught in the middle between my wife and my sister."
Joe's Story:

"My wife will hardly talk with my sister anymore. Actually, I can't blame her. My sister has twin boys and an older one who's 12. We have three kids too. Our oldest is 15 and has so many problems. I don't even know the names of all of them. He's in a wheelchair and can't go to the bathroom by himself. We also have two younger boys who are five and eight. They're a handful, but they're healthy.

My sister calls here and goes on and on about how busy she is, and my wife just listens. She usually puts my sister on speaker so she can get things done around the house. My sister is a sweetheart, but she's always been a complainer. When I get home, my wife tells me how frustrated she is. My sister has no clue what busy is in our world. Of course my sister is busy. We all know that. It's hard for any family to find enough time in the day to get things done, including cooking dinner, helping with homework and driving kids to practice. But if they had the additional responsibilities we have, they'd think again.

I feel alone and frustrated because I can't support my wife enough, and I can't shut my sister up. If my sister came over and had to feed, bathe and dress my 15-year-old son every day, not to mention clean his bag and feed tubes, she'd be busier than she could've ever imagined. And she'd go crazy if she had to spend half the day calling therapists, doctors and pharmacists, not to mention the insurance companies that make us write letters for everything. While I care about my sister, she makes it hard for me to defend her. She could use a reality check."

My Thoughts: Sometimes an activity that usually takes a few hours can turn into something much longer. One example is an emergency room visit that turns into an overnight, multiple-night or several-week hospital stay. It's both exhausting and rewarding. We can't expect everyone to understand our lives.

"I don't feel alone, and I think it's because of my son."

Sophie's Story:

"I never really felt alone. In fact, from the start, I believe I needed something in my life that was meaningful. I was alone and lonely before having this child. I believe God gave me this child to be my teacher. He teaches me how to be patient and to really care about something. When I'm alone, I feel a sort of peace that I haven't felt before having this precious child. I don't feel alone. He's my teacher. We need each other."

"I feel alone in public."

Troy's Story:

"When my child's behavior is out of control and I don't know what to do to control her, I feel very alone. I don't handle it well, especially in public. I don't even want to look around to see who may be watching. All I can think is that others feel sorry for me or think I'm a terrible parent for having a child who seems so out of control, screaming and flailing her arms. I learned to put it in perspective. I say to myself, 'If they only knew how sweet this little girl is when she feels good.' That helps me remember that this child is communicating with me, not them. I'm the only one who needs to listen."

"I felt alone when my husband and I didn't agree."

Mary's Story:

"I used to feel alone when my husband and I couldn't listen to each other about ideas we had for our child. I would stumble upon a new idea or treatment. However, after a few minutes of conversation, he would shut down with frustration. He was unwilling to try something new for fear it was unnecessary, too risky or not going to work. Finally, we came to a point where we just couldn't live together. His family was furious with us. They said things like 'Everyone has marital problems and disagreements. And all children are difficult to deal with. Why can't you guys do it?' They bought me books on discipline, relaxing and talking with your child. I remember reading the titles and screaming in my head, 'Are you kidding me?' I felt like doing a reality show on TV so they could walk in our shoes for a few weeks. Eventually, my husband and I talked instead of screamed about how we could handle challenging and rough days. Counseling helped.

Once we agreed to communicate and listen, the 'all alone' feeling was replaced with relief. We still disagree, but we work together to manage the rough days. We seem closer. When his family criticizes us, I ask them if they'd like to move in for a few weeks while I take a vacation. They usually respond with silence."

"Alone is when I feel like my child's only friend."

Jessica's Story:

"Every year we go to Cedar Point Amusement Park. It's a good day. But in my heart, there's more sadness than happiness. Jack loves to go with me, and he's excited that I'm his riding partner. Each year I realize, once again, that I'm my child's only friend. Although he gets along with everyone, there's really no one in his life he can spend the day going places with. Others will say, 'You're so lucky your son wants to go with you.' Or they'll ask, 'Did you have fun?' No one really understands how it feels to be your child's most important—and only—friend. Every year, we have a good day at the park, and Jack loves it. It's a rough day in my heart, though, knowing my son does things without a friend."

"Alone is 24/7 worry."

Nina's Story:

"I feel most alone knowing others can't understand the

extent of my worry. Everyone says they worry about their kids, but not like this. It's hard to explain the difference between my worry and the worry of other parents who have typical kids. My child Randy is a 5-foot-9-inch, 150-pound teenager. He looks like a grown man, but he's childlike and trusting. He makes bad decisions and is easily influenced by others.

Last summer, while in the neighbor's yard, he jumped off their garage roof into the pool below. Lucky, he didn't break his legs or neck. The neighbor kids dared each other to do it, and Randy actually did. He's incredibly trusting. I worry that he's unable to say no, resist peer pressure or fight for himself. I also worry that, at any time or place, someone could take advantage of his vulnerability and purposely capitalize on that for selfish reasons.

Will he ever know the difference between real and pretend friends? Slice it any way you want. This kind of 24/7 worry makes me feel truly alone."

"I feel alone when I get jealous."

TJ's Story:

"As a dad, I notice when other kids achieve milestones two or three steps ahead of him—and I see him struggle. I'm actually happy for other kids who can do things automatically like swallow, sing, hold a spoon and ask questions. When I let myself feel jealous of what other kids can do, I just hurt and feel very alone."

"I feel sad watching Laura get left behind."

Lauren's Story:

"The older Laura gets, the more distance there is between her and her peers. She became more distant from kids her age during her teenage years. I feel alone when it seems no one else can see how far Laura has fallen behind."

"I feel very alone and angry when my family just doesn't get it."

Tammy's Story:

"My family, who doesn't spend a lot of time with my Tony, tells me that he'll be better and I'll eventually find a cure for this. When I hear that, I feel like I'm living in another world because they'll never understand. I say, 'No, this is life. Tony will never, ever get better.' They just don't get it."

"I feel alone when others judge my situation."

Tina's Story:

"My son can be very stubborn when something changes like a schedule, a teacher or even the weather—if he didn't expect it. When we're in a store, he has a hard time if the line is long. Sounds, smells, noises, lights or too many people can bother him. When others overhear me trying to coax him into leaving the store or staying by me, they often comment with remarks like 'Wow! You can't get him to change his mind. He must be a difficult one.' What they don't know is that my child is unable to talk, so he acts out his thoughts and feelings. I know he makes loud noises and calls attention to himself. The bigger the crowd, the more alone I feel."

"Feeling lonely at the playground makes me sad for her."

Jake's Story:

"My daughter begs me to take her to the park. I watch her and I can see she can't climb on the playground equipment or enjoy what's there without being lifted up or carried from one thing to another. I feel completely alone as I watch her and I think, 'She really can't do anything here.' I'm reminded that things other people do so naturally are impossible for her."

"I feel alone when the guilt hits me because
I'm not always patient with Lily."

Dan's Story:

"It drives me crazy when I'm waiting and waiting because everything takes so long. I want to scream, 'Hurry up!' Potty training and bedtime routines took almost a year. Brushing her teeth takes over an hour and getting dressed takes over 40 minutes, not counting the shoes. I feel alone, waiting and waiting. I also feel selfish because I want time for myself. But there's no time left at the end of the day. I'm exhausted and ashamed that I'm frustrated with Lily when she can't move faster."

4 **Feeling Alone** *A Look Back*

Feeling alone was the most common observation of the parents and caregivers who shared their experiences. Their description of this powerful feeling of isolation isn't the same as being lonely. Many parents and caregivers explain that there are a lot of people in their lives who love and support them and their children, and they're not lonely. But they still feel alone.

Feeling alone seems linked to the exhaustion and disappointment of not knowing the answers to medical or mental health questions, believing that others can't begin to understand the level of your fear or worry, or repeating the unanswerable "what if" questions that flood your mind.

Parents of children with special needs aren't necessarily special parents. Most of us are everyday people who need what everyone else needs, namely love, understanding, encouragement and support. Collectively, we're a powerful group that connects and understands each other as we appreciate and witness each miracle on this unplanned journey. As we connect to each other, we are less alone.

"It is clear to me that each child given is a blessing and a gift who teaches us so much about ourselves, others and what is truly important in this life. Kids with special needs are some of God's best gifts."

—*Cindi DiGeronimo,*
Mother of 8, Grandmother of 37

5 Loving this Child as a Couple and Listening to the Tone of 'We'

MARRIED COUPLES AND COUPLES IN domestic partnerships were asked what they would tell couples who were just beginning their journey, so they, too, could keep their relationships strong. Embracing the New Normal as a couple and a family is a critically important goal. Talking honestly about what your expectations are before *and* after a diagnosis can unite couples. Couples who share their stories provide valuable tips for those new to this situation.

"If he can do it independently, we both let him."
Amelia and Larry's Story:

"Our suggestion to other parents is to do your best to treat your child as if he or she doesn't have a disability. Together, you can try to make this child as independent as possible. Look beyond the disability and focus on your child's *ability*. Our son, Jacob, has a unique personality, just like our other two children, and he is more typical than not. We let him try all kinds of things so he can learn just like anyone else. He constantly surprises us with his independence. And he shows all of us how challenges that seem impossible can be overcome. Sometimes he is more independent with his dad. With me, he wants things done for him. As his mom, I try not to let him slide on this. I try not to be the parent who keeps doing for him the things we know he can do independently. If he can do something for one parent, we encourage him to do it with both."

"Divorce doesn't mean you can't provide stability."

John and Joni's Story:

"We had to find a way to have a healthy relationship for our kids. We're divorced, but realize that all four of our kids need stability, especially Ryan, who has difficulty learning, socializing and tolerating change. He needs more stability from us because more things are challenging for him. All our kids depend on us to show them how to handle challenges, conflict and change. So if all we did were challenge each other and constantly point the finger—instead of figuring out what to do—our kids would learn that kind of behavior. When we're hostile and angry at each other, they feel it. They copy us. So we decided how we were going to act together, based on what we wanted our children to learn from us, and we manage to do it."

"God finally touched the other half of our marriage."

Ella and Tom's Story:

"God has always given me strength. But after we had our child with special needs, he has given Tom strength. My husband started praying when he figured out we couldn't fix our child's condition. It was so hard in the beginning, and I was always more at peace than Tom was. He was always frustrated and quiet. One day, Tom asked me how I calmed myself. I told him I pray for hope and doing so calms me. I don't know how he prays, but he does."

"We decide together."

Jac and Teri's Story:

"Agree with your spouse about how to get your child involved. We learned early to get Joseph involved in everything possible right off the bat. There are different groups for children with special needs. We enrolled him in music, sports, horseback riding and story groups so he could be with other kids and participate as much as possible. The first two baseball seasons, he sat on the field and played in the dirt instead of paying attention to the game. One of us would stand near him to keep him safe from the ball. We agreed that he was improving, but in very small steps. He was tolerating the sounds, movement and being on the field with the other kids. By the third season, he was standing up and stopping the ball. He plays catch now too. It would've been easy to give up and say, 'Forget baseball because he isn't really playing.' But we didn't."

"Keep it together."

Erin and Gino's Story:

"You have to keep it together, *together.*"

My Thoughts: Listen to what your partner is saying instead of thinking ahead about what you want to say next. In this order: LISTEN, THINK and then SPEAK your mind.

"Our marriage is real."

Brian and Madison's Story:

"After 12 years of marriage, we realized we were emotionally worn down from the constant medical crises. We learned how to rely on each other more, reach out to each other more and accept that we weren't going to be on the same emotional page all the time. We learned to rely on each other for everything from offering support and a shoulder to cry on to being a best friend. Our child with special needs made our marriage real. Our son is ours, on the good days and on the tough ones. We have to allow each other to be honest about it all."

"Talk, talk, talk!"

Rudy and Jan's Story:

"Talk, talk, talk—together. And when one of you freaks

out, talk again and again, and pull it all back together—as a couple."

My Thoughts: There are good days and bad days. You and your partner aren't always going to have the same one.

"I love that girl."

Peggy and Todd's Story:

"Being a guy, I never thought I'd be involved in a decision to terminate a pregnancy or take into consideration the women's choice issue. But it happened when Peggy was about four months pregnant. We were asked to meet with the doctor to discuss the test results. They showed markers indicating the baby was at risk for medical problems. We were in a small office, listening to the list of possible scenarios. The doctor described these horrible 'invisible' problems and suggested options. He mentioned adoption, live-in healthcare and abortion. These were words I couldn't connect with having a baby. They all sounded terrible. I wasn't prepared at all. Was he guessing or was he serious? Did this doctor have hang-ups about us not being married? Did he believe an unwed couple shouldn't have a baby? How bad was it? I looked at Peggy and had no idea what she was thinking. She said nothing and cried the entire meeting. I remember trying to listen, but my mind was spinning. I was sweating and my skin felt like it was on fire. Is this about not wanting to or not being able to handle a child who may be sick or different?

On the drive home, I wanted to talk, but I couldn't get the words out. As I continued to say nothing, Peggy cried even harder. That was terrible, too. Later, I said something, just to open the door to a conversation. I had gotten a few words out before she stopped me and said, 'I don't want you to leave, but if you want to go, go now. My baby and I are going nowhere.' I remember that exact moment. I couldn't speak. I just stood there with tears streaming down my face. I never considered leaving. Who knows what was going to happen?

A few months later, our son was born early. Now I understand what the doctor was talking about. And he was right. My son has many problems, and his life is filled with tubes, heart monitors, doctor visits, lab tests and medications. But you should see what my little guy does. Every time he squeezes my finger, he looks right at me like he knows what he's doing. He knows me. And he has a sense that he's OK. How did we make this decision? Peggy made our decision the second the doctor started talking. I love that girl."

"I'm kind of a jerk when I'm frustrated."

Jim and Rachael's Story:

"Rachael was a great catch. My buddies tease me about how lucky I am to have a wife who cooks and is beautiful. They joke and constantly tell me I 'married up.' Last year, I went with the guys on a weekend fishing trip. I called Rachael and must have been a jerk during our phone conversation.

After the trip, my best friend called me out. He asked me why I was so loud, critical and demanding when I spoke with Rachael. Guys don't talk like that, so I knew I must've been stupid. At the time, I didn't think I was that bad. But after hearing what he had to say, I guess I was. I'm not always fair when I'm frustrated. I get critical and say things I don't even mean. I listen to myself now, and I try not to take my frustration out on her. It's the stress of not knowing what's going on with this kid that makes me crazy. I know Rachael hates it when I run my mouth. Hearing from a close friend that I was a jerk wasn't easy, but I was grateful. That conversation probably saved our marriage. I finally shut up and started listening to my wife. It's hard for me, but it's hard for her, too."

"Build your expectations and future lives together."

Joan and Tommy's Story:

"We think couples in this situation should talk about marriage. What does it mean to each of you? What are your expectations about family life? Your finances? Have you considered that the empty nest part of the marriage may never happen? Keep your reality, hopes and dreams in check so you can build your life together."

"It's better to say, 'I'm sad and life isn't fair.'"

Jill and Calvin's Story:

"What would we tell a couple who recently found out their child has special needs? First, both of you are grieving over what could or should have been. If you share with one another what was initially expected and what each of you believes the reality is now, you'll be able to understand where your spouse is coming from—and vice versa.

The first step is hard. It's like no one wants to say it. But it's better to say you're sad and that life isn't fair. If you don't say it, you may feel it inside and then take it out on each other. Couples like us are under a lot of stress. And sometimes, being strong means admitting you don't feel so strong. Talking and listening lets you see the situation from both sides."

My Thoughts: Commit to resolving a challenge or problem as a team – from the SAME side of the table. Put the problem on the other side as you reason, talk and listen. Retaliate against the challenge or problem, not each other.

"Get on the same page with your spouse about the answers to your child's tough questions."

Jenny and Marcus's Story:

"Give each other permission to challenge each other. There will be many issues that other families don't have. Parents with typical children won't have to explain to their kids why they can't get married, drive a car, have children or go everywhere with their friends. Other parents won't have their 8-year-old asking, 'Mommy, am I broken?' Or their 15-year-old asking, 'Why can't I play on the football team?' Or their 13-year-old asking, 'Why do I have to take this medication and sleep with this machine every night? It keeps me from going to sleepovers with the other kids.' Don't ignore talking with your child about his or her challenges. However, be sure to discuss your child's challenges and concerns with your spouse beforehand, so the two of you are on the same page with your answers."

"Get on the same page about your other kids."

Roger and Terri's Story:

"We have four children. Our oldest child, Derrick, has special needs due to a complication at birth. He was the only twin who survived. Our younger children are able to reason and socialize at a higher level than Derrick, so in some ways, Derrick is the youngest.

We learned to talk to our other kids about Derrick's developmental and medical challenges. We always listen to what they think and feel about our family's situation. We realize that while they really love their brother, sometimes they want to do things without him. For example, last year, we went on a ski trip with our other three children, and Derrick stayed with my parents.

Advice we would give to new parents is to pay attention to your other kids and their interests, too. Don't miss watching their activities. Try not to allow your children to be the caregivers to your child with special needs so you can get a break. They can help out. But it isn't their responsibility to make sure your child gets a bath, medications or dinner. Also, allow your other kids to express their honest feelings. We found that our kids are hesitant to complain because they think their problems are small compared to Derrick's. We let them know that anything they're concerned about is important, and we're here to listen."

My Thoughts: Many couples have goals for their children with special needs, but they aren't the same goals. Talk. Understand what common goals the two of you have for your child, from education and work to financial needs and future living arrangements. And then plan together.

5 Loving this Child as a Couple and Listening to the Tone of 'We' *A Look Back*

Couples acknowledge that it isn't easy to manage the challenges of caring for a child with special needs, especially when there are other children in the family. It's important to maintain a healthy relationship with all your children. Let them know that their interests and problems are important, too. Encourage open, honest communication.

Our challenges as parents and spouses encourage us to realize each other's individual strengths. As we do, we get stronger together. The stronger we are as a couple, the better we can deal with our challenges. Be mindful that although we're individuals, we're also a "we." Plan ahead. Spend time together to have fun, without talking about the kids, finances, work or medical concerns.

"Disabilities can become abilities that enable a child to flourish. It's a matter of finding – and then cultivating – the best environment so that each unique child is nurtured along the way."

—*Mark A. Foglietti, D.O.,*
Cosmetic Surgery Institute Northeast, Ohio

6 Responding to Other People and the Shocking Things They Do or Say

FOR THOSE WHO HAVEN'T INTERACTED with a child with special needs—or the parent of one—there may be uncertainty, even anxiousness, over what to do or say. Most caregivers and parents of children with special needs understand the reasons for these concerns and eagerly use any interaction between their children and others as a teaching moment. With our guidance, many people come to realize that our children are more *like* other children than they are different.

In the following narratives, parents and caregivers share their experiences and responses to those who care about and want to know our children. These same parents and caregivers also touch on their experiences with those who behave judgmentally and hurtfully with words, glaring stares and reckless comments.

"The Easter egg hunt I'll never forget."

Vanessa's Story:

"I remember when Jerry was about 7 years old. I took him to his first Easter egg hunt at our local recreation center. Most of the children participating were healthy children. I helped Jerry walk and gather eggs because he didn't have the strength to bend down and stand back up. Another parent watched me help Jerry and became hostile. She accused my son of cheating. She protested loudly in front of him and the crowd, claiming that my helping him was unfair to the other children. I was shocked. Anyone could see his limitations. His arms are bone-skinny. And his posture is stiff and his balance impaired as he lifts his feet high in the air with every step. She may have assumed he couldn't understand her anger, insensitivity and verbal protest.

She couldn't have been more wrong. Jerry was devastated to be accused of cheating and breaking the rules. He would never cheat. In fact, now at 17 years old, he still doesn't tolerate rule breaking, whether by his own doing or by others. I was devastated, humiliated and embarrassed for him. I felt embarrassed and angry, believing that no one at that event could understand how much encouragement it took just to convince him to go to the Easter egg hunt that day. I don't know if that lady remembers her protests, but Jerry does. I could never convince him to participate in another Easter egg hunt."

"FAIR really is a four-letter word."

Lyle's Story:

"My child was at a summer recreational sport camp, playing kickball. At age 12, she needed help to walk, talk, kick the ball and run the bases. The coach would stop the ball and hold it in front of the plate as she tried to kick it. She had to kick a few times to make contact, but she did it. I was happy to have the day off to see her play with other kids. While sitting in the stands, I overheard two women discussing whether it was fair to help one kid and not the others. I knew they were talking about my kid. They were debating this issue, comparing her to the other kids who seemed able to kick the ball and run on their own. As I listened, I wondered how they defined the word 'fair'. I didn't ask because I didn't want to know."

"I'm more surprised by adults than anyone else."

Dan's Story:

"I learned that adults can be much more critical and judgmental than children. One day, my two sons were at a bus stop. Timmy's a typical 16-year-old. His twin brother, Matthew, is in a wheelchair and is paralyzed on his right side. It was something that happened before birth because, together, they took up too much room.

At the bus stop, another parent was making comments to Timmy about his shaved head, dark tan and tattoo, as well as something about his shirt. It wasn't fun and games, and the adult wasn't joking with Tim.

He clearly didn't approve of Tim's look and was nasty.

When they got home, Matthew and Timmy shared with me what had happened. They explained that they just smiled and pretended to be OK with this man's comments. However, my sons were clearly angry and told me that if this person ever did that again, Tim would knock him down while Matthew rolled over him with his chair.

Of course that wouldn't be the right way to handle the situation, and I couldn't see my boys doing anything like that. However, some people could use the message. I wonder if that guy is aware that Timmy helps bathe and tutor his brother almost every night. He even cuts up Matthew's food. By the way, Timmy's tattoo reads, 'My twin is the BETTER half.' I didn't want Tim getting a tattoo at his age, but I couldn't say no to one like that. I find it unbelievable how some adults are such poor role models around children. Sometimes I want to go find that guy and wish upon him what we have to deal with here. Then again, I wouldn't want a sweet child like mine to have to deal with that kind of stupid."

"We agreed to disagree about her comments."

Janis's Story:

"My mother-in-law asked me, 'You hire people to raise your children?' At the time, I remember wanting her to be a part of our lives. And I certainly wanted her to get to know our children, especially Jenny, our child with special needs. I freely invited her to visit and spend time with us. But each time she did, she had something sarcastic to say about our sitters and house cleaner. My husband, Dan, and I argued about her comments. He'd tell me to ignore her because she's always been the type to say something about everyone and everything. I'd had enough, and I wanted her to stop.

Realizing we weren't on the same page with our feelings, my husband and I agreed to disagree. Nevertheless, Dan and I knew we needed the help. We just couldn't do it all ourselves. Dan's mother continued to say, 'I never had to hire a sitter to raise my kids or someone to clean my house.' I remember feeling guilty and inadequate because I couldn't do it all. But I was exhausted.

Finally, Dan agreed that we should talk with her about it. With the three of us in the room, he initiated the conversation. For a full ten minutes, my husband talked and talked, but said essentially nothing. So I stepped up and said, 'I'm exhausted and I need help. And it kills me when you make negative comments about it. Please come here and be the grandmother and not my supervisor.' After that conversation, his mother never said a word about it in front of me. Even to this day, she keeps her mouth shut. I have to say, she's a good grandma. The kids love her."

My Thoughts: It's perfectly OK to ask someone to talk behind your back so you don't have to hear their negative comments. Consider their negative thoughts a self-reflection.

"Sorry?"

JoAnn's Story:

"When people see my child and say, 'Oh, I'm sorry,' I just don't know how to take that comment."

"I wanted to say, 'No, you don't know.'"

Linda's Story:

"If one more person says, 'I know, I have teenagers too,' I'm going to scream. I know teenagers think independently, make poor decisions and disobey rules. I know this. But when your teenager makes independent decisions to stop taking medications and receiving chemotherapy treatments, refuses life-saving surgeries or becomes too sick to eat or drink independently, the worry is unbearable. I learned that the heartache of having a teenager with special needs is much different from everyday life with a 'typical' teenager. I'm not worried that my teenager's decisions will prevent her from making the cheerleading squad. I'm worried my teenager will make a decision that'll prevent her from staying alive."

My Thoughts: It's difficult to hear others say, 'I know exactly how you feel' or 'What happened?' It's better to hear, 'You have a precious child' or 'This isn't easy for you.' Keep in mind that most people try to say the right thing. It's difficult for everyone.

"Clef pallet made my son look different, but
his friends didn't let that matter."

Jerry's Story:

"We had our baby, and it was obvious he didn't look normal. He had a clef pallet, just like the ones pictured in magazine ads. Our baby was just as cute as the kids in the pictures. He had a ton of black hair, but his face was split in half at the mouth. And there was no hiding it. The moment he was born, the doctors and nurses rushed him out of the room before my wife and I could even see him. That scared me more than anything, although I knew he was alive because I could hear him screaming. Eventually, they had a big group meeting in our room to explain the situation. Finally, they let us hold him. I think the doctors and nurses were more shaken than we were. Now I realize this was probably because they knew that years of physical and emotional pain were ahead of us.

I've been in law enforcement for years and have seen a lot of bad things, but I've never cried in front of people. My son changed that. I cried like a baby every time I saw him all wrapped up, stitched and just feeling miserable. We had to do it because his lips, mouth, jaw and teeth were messed up. He had over 20 surgeries to correct the bone structure. Once that was done, many cosmetic surgeries followed. I took him everywhere with me, except to work. When people asked, stared and glared, I'd say, 'It hurts, but he's brave and he's letting us fix it.' The best example of my son's resilience was the surgery on his lips. They were sewn shut for eight weeks to cause scar tissue to grow. They used the scar tissue to make his lips thicker. I still can't believe he figured out how to eat a steak through a straw. Genius. He's had to deal with stares, glares, mean comments and pain from total strangers. He has missed school, holidays and vacations because of surgeries.

Despite all his challenges, he's smart and fun. And he has a great group of friends. He looks good, too. His friends have known him since kindergarten and are used to his slurred speech and swollen face after surgery. My son has never had to defend himself because his friends do it for him. I tell his friends to be careful and deal with others without throwing a punch. My son drives, gets good grades and goes to concerts and school functions. He's applying to colleges and has plans to be a math teacher. He worries about finding a girlfriend who will accept that he looks slightly different. I tell my son all the time, the real problem is him. He's too picky about girls. He'll learn."

"It's OK to ask, but ..."

Jill's Story:

"A woman asked me, 'What's wrong with her?' I thought to myself, 'How can I answer that? Should I even try to answer that question?' It would've been better had she asked, 'What kind of special needs does your child have?'"

"Questions, questions."

Ruth's Story:

"There was a couple standing next to my son, Nate, and me at the deli counter. Out of the corner of my eye, I could see the man staring, maybe trying to figure out what was different about Nate. The man turned toward me and asked, 'Do you feel like you have been punished with him?' I must have appeared surprised by his question because his wife immediately interrupted him and said, 'Honey, please, don't ask any questions.' Then she turned toward me and said, 'Don't mind my husband. He doesn't do well with diversity.' I stood there, speechless. I ignored both of them and went about my business."

My Thoughts: Regardless of whether the comments or questions we encounter are caring or reckless, our response will set the tone. Sometimes the best thing to say is nothing. Silence is heard loud and clear.

"It took me a few weeks to answer the question."

Jay's Story:

"When I was a kid and before I was married, I hung out with bad asses. We had fun, drank a lot and got into fights. None of us wanted to grow up, and we were stupid. Now I'm a father. I have real responsibilities. My son is my world, although he isn't normal like other kids. I don't mean he isn't normal. But you know, he can't go out on his own and get married, take care of himself, drive or stuff like that. I remember running into one of my old buddies, and he asked me if I thought God was punishing me for all the stuff we did. I was stunned at the question, but I really thought about it. I called him back a few weeks later to answer him. I told him, 'No, I don't think I'm being punished.' My buddy and I talked about all the trouble we got into as kids—and even in our twenties—and how we both had to grow up once we had families. I told him I believe I have a son with special needs because this is how God asked me to contribute to the world and become a better parent and person.

I'm not a religious man, but I believe God picked my son to be my teacher and me, his student. Yes, my friend asked a harsh question, but he's my buddy and I know he cares. He expected me to feel angry. My friends all have older kids now and can go do whenever they want. To tell you the truth, I don't want to. I'm perfectly fine staying here at home with my son and my wife. My friend and I talked about how both of us have changed and that we both still have a lot to learn. It was good."

"My child is THAT child at church."

Betty's Story:

"My daughter sits in a wheelchair in the aisle at church. Her legs are tied to the footrests, and she moans when the music starts to play. Why do I bother to take her with me? I love church and feel peaceful when I pray. I have a wonderful relationship with God. And it's my right to attend church and bring my child with me, just like every other family. Most people are kind, loving and have always been friendly. But there are also the annoying ones. Some people and their comments are more than just rude. They actually question my daughter's right to live or ever appear in public.

At times, I struggle to hold back tears or the urge to

punch anyone who is glaring, gawking, rolling their eyes in disgust or saying uncaring things about my child. I try to put the worst comments out of my mind. Some of the worst are: 'Why do you bring her here?' 'Does she even understand or get anything out of church?' and 'God must give you special strength to handle this problem.' Labeling my child a 'problem' is bad, but what's even worse are some of the looks on people's faces. Their looks are so obvious. They may as well just say, 'Why did you ruin your life with such a burden? Why keep an unproductive person alive?'

Why do I bring her to church? I do because she loves the music, feels peaceful and moans when she's happy. Others may have aborted, not fed her or put her in a home. I choose to love her and see her as my beautiful child, not as a burden, life-ender or problem that I've been punished with. I wish the people who don't agree with me would just ignore us. But for those who are accepting and unsure of what to say, try something like, 'Have a great holiday.' 'She looks pretty today.' 'I heard her singing again.' 'Nice to see you again.' To kindness like that, I would smile and say, 'Thank you.'"

"I make a point to say, 'Thank you for being so kind.'"
My Story:
"My daughter sits with a group of kids her age in the student section at the high school games. She's happy when she feels a part of the group. I take pictures from the stands of her cheering, laughing and really having fun. Most students in the group clearly know her challenges. They also know that she will not be a high school cheerleader or play a high school

sport. However, these kids invite her and take the time to get to know her. They don't exclude her because she needs help walking up the bleachers, speaking clearly or understanding the game. The group decided to accept her as one of their own with kindness and patience. I tell them how much I appreciate their kindness. I really think it warms their hearts, too, to see her laughing, clapping and fitting right in."

"The word 'retarded' should be erased."

Jill's Story:

"I was at a soccer game watching my oldest of three children play. I was sitting on the sideline with my son and daughter when another mom asked, 'Is your daughter retarded?' That word gets under my skin. What does it mean? Is she asking me if my child can think, hear or play? My daughter, Emily, has Down syndrome. She's mainstreamed in school and plays soccer. She is slower to learn some things. But once she gets it, she remembers it, just like any other kid. I asked the lady what *retarded* means. I went on to say, 'I don't use the term, so I'm unfamiliar with its meaning.' She reworded her question and we began talking about Emily in a respectful way. Or should I say, we discussed Emily like anyone would discuss any child. I believe that, by the end of the conversation, she understood that Emily has the ability to learn, play and communicate like others, but at a slower pace. I wish the word 'retarded' was erased from our vocabulary and not used as a general adjective. Using labels as adjectives or nouns isn't fair or nice. In fact, it's hurtful. Our kids have no defense."

"When people see my child as a disability ..."

Mary's Story:

"It's difficult when others see my child and, they only see a disability. I was in church, holding my 3-year-old child, and the lady sitting in front of me turned around and asked, 'Do you think he knows you?' I said, 'Of course he knows me. I'm probably the only thing he knows.' It's obvious to everyone that my son, Tyler, is blind. I'm crying even now, explaining this story—even though it's ten years later—because I still can't believe the question. How could anyone ask a mother if her child knows her? Yes, my son is visually impaired, but he can feel, talk and think. And he knows a lot of people. Looking back, I don't think this lady was trying to be mean or insensitive, but her question sure was. So I answered it loudly, right then and there."

"I stood there thinking, 'You just said that?'"

Karl's Story:

"I was outside chasing our garbage cans, which were blowing around in the street. A neighbor approached me and asked me how Sammy was doing. Sammy is our 5-year-old son with muscular dystrophy. I started telling him how frustrated Sammy is because he wants to run and play, like the other kids, but his muscles aren't strong enough to hold him up. Winters are long for him. We bring him outside when the weather's nice. We put him in his stand so he can be upright and throw the ball around a little bit. My neighbor explained that he works nights and his wife works days, so he's home with his 2- and 3-year-old kids. He then said, 'Well, at least you don't have to run around chasing him all day. And you can get a break if you sit him in front of the TV.'

I just stood there, stunned by his comment and certain he didn't understand what I'd said. So I repeated, 'Well, Sammy would love to run around, but he just can't. I wish he could. That would be awesome.' This guy just kept going on. He said, 'Well, at least you get a break and don't have to worry about him getting into everything. It drives me crazy when there are toys everywhere.' With that, I'd heard enough. I was shocked, stunned and angry. I looked right into his eyes and asked, 'Are you some kind of idiot?' He paused—and then continued on with his complaints about how his kids are nonstop and run all over the house. I walked away thinking, 'Unbelievable, just unbelievable.'"

6 Responding to Other People and the Shocking Things They Do or Say
A Look Back

Most people who behave insensitively around our children aren't acting out of malice, but rather ignorance and awkwardness. Even so, these uncomfortable encounters can be embarrassing, hurtful and even infuriating. We can help these individuals interact with our children by sharing accurate and honest information about our situation. We don't have to share too much information. But sharing some often helps those outside our situation gain insight, awareness and a perspective that provides a better understanding of our children. And while these encounters may stretch our patience to its limits, people usually respond favorably and become aware that our children do not misunderstand the stares, glares, rude comments and rejection of others.

Parents and caregivers admit that no matter what we do, there will always be people who shock us with their careless, hurtful or mean behavior. In response, we can either retaliate or walk away. Unfortunately, some narrow minds can't be opened, so ignoring the person's comments and walking away is oftentimes the best option.

We're a powerful group. We set the tone. We talk with others to educate them. We teach others as they watch us love our children. And we provide the most comfortable situation possible so others can get to know and interact with our amazing kids. Fortunately, most people we meet along our journey move forward with us.

In the next chapter, parents and caregivers talk about the countless people who embrace the joy we already know.

"If we take the time out of our busy lives, we can all learn valuable life lessons from these kids. They do not judge people by skin color, ethnicity, religion, size or shape. They are friendly, caring and outgoing. And they genuinely want to get to know you for who you are—on the inside. Each child I have worked with who has a disability has touched my life and has made me a better person. As I reflect after each event we host, I soak in the joy and wonder who benefited more—them or me?"

—*John Zakel Jr., Director of Special Olympics Young Athletes Cleveland*

7 Embracing the Good and Those Who Care

T HE BROTHERS AND SISTERS OF CHILDREN with special needs have a profound understanding of what caring for and loving these amazing kids is all about. Some are younger, some older and some are fellow twins or triplets. These siblings often refer to themselves as the *other kids*. They take a back seat when the family is attending to an overwhelming medical, physical or emotional challenge of a sibling with special needs. Other times, however, the spotlight is on them as they excel in sports, academics and other opportunities their brothers or sisters with special needs may not have.

Still, there are many individuals who have no connection. They aren't family members of a child with special needs. They could easily ignore the whole topic, but they don't. They're people of all ages who willingly take the time to get to know our children, establish friendships and share their lives, skills and kindness during lunch times, sports and social events. They enjoy our kids. The brothers and sisters of children with special needs, as well as countless others who choose to learn, understand and take the opportunity to embrace our children and their abilities, are immeasurably appreciated.

Read on for stories about how embracing the good is shared by everyone through contagious acts of kindness.

"My friends are her friends, but in a different way."

Daniel's Story (age 18):

"My little sister has seizures and is slow to learn things. She doesn't know who's a good person and who's isn't. She thinks everyone's good. We're only two years apart, but it seems like she's still 10 years old or something. I love that I'm her big brother. A lot of my teenage friends hang out at our house. Over the years, they've come to know her. She smiles, seems happy, gives them high-fives and thinks they're all good kids. If any one of my friends found out someone were hurting my sister, they'd be devastated, angry and really hurt. We all love her. And my friends are her friends, but in a different way. She always seems positive and can come up with real solutions to problems. Sometimes I sit and talk with her just to take a break from how hectic school, sports and girls can be. She constantly shows me how lucky I am not to have seizures, medications, blood tests and surgeries all the time. Unfortunately, she spends a lot of her summers and school breaks at the hospital. She's brave, courageous, tough and so special to me. I hope I never lose her."

My Thoughts: No one knows how many tomorrows we have left, but we have today. Today we can chose to listen and speak up for those who can't.

"It's like watching a movie and you're the only one in the room who knows the ending is fabulous."

Julia's Story (age 13):

"I figured out that my friends were afraid of my sister. My sister's nice, but she's different. She can't keep up with other kids. She had brain cancer when she was 2 years old, and the surgeries, chemotherapy and radiation treatments make it hard for her to learn things and talk like other kids. Considering all she has gone through, she's pretty smart. She's also fun to be around. She laughs, plays games with us and likes to go out to eat. We're both teenagers, and I wanted my friends to get to know her. That way, I wouldn't have to pick between hanging out with them and hanging out with my sister. She doesn't have a lot of friends, so I started inviting my friends over, one at a time, to be with my sister and me.

Imagine watching a movie that you know has a fabulous ending—without being allowed to tell anyone how the movie ends. Instead, you'd have to sit and watch it with each of your friends. When it was over, your friend would say, 'Wow! That was so good. Why didn't you tell me the ending was this awesome? And you would say, 'I knew you'd love the movie, but I couldn't tell you how it ended because it wouldn't have been the same. You had to see it and experience it for yourself.'

That's what happens when my friends get to know my sister. They love her by the end of the night. But they have to be with her and experience her for themselves, just like watching an awesome movie. After that, they aren't afraid of her. They find out she's just a girl. She isn't fragile. She can laugh, make decisions and be with us in a group. Of course she isn't exactly like us. But in some ways, she's better. My sister doesn't lie. She doesn't get jealous or talk behind your back like some of the girls do. She's innocent and kind. Once my friends get to know her, they protect her like I do from people who can take advantage of her. It's really good when that happens. The girls who can't figure this out aren't real friends."

My Thoughts: Many brothers and sisters of children with special needs develop intuitive skills about friendships early on. They understand that a true friend inspires you, doesn't judge and reminds you not to judge yourself too harshly.

"At first, I hid the fact that Travis was my brother."
Rae Ann's Story (age 14):

"My brother, Travis, has a lot of special needs. He's in a wheelchair and can't speak clearly. I know what he's trying to say, but not many people understand him, except my family and his aide at school. Or so I thought. Travis was already in the eleventh grade when I started at the high school. I was afraid to let other kids know Travis was my brother because I wanted to make friends, and I was afraid other kids would avoid me. I didn't see Travis that much at school because he spends his day in the resource room, and my classes are all over the building. But after school, I noticed different kids talking to him. Some would grab chairs and sit next to him so Travis could see them at his level. My brother seemed to know everyone, even the cool kids. He smiled, and they talked with him and gave him high-fives. The basketball coach even gave him a varsity jersey. I discovered that Travis has a lot of friends. And they all talk with him. I felt bad about hiding the fact that he's my brother. Eventually, I told people about Travis, and I actually met people through him. I had to learn that I could be myself and, at the same time, Travis's sister. I hope he never knows I was hiding from being his sister because he'd never hide from being my brother."

"My granddaughter has problems I'd never heard of."
Jennet's Story:

"My granddaughter is always at the hospital for some type of infection. I really don't know all of what's involved. Although my son tells me some of it, he doesn't tell me everything so I don't worry. Like it or not, I worry anyway. My granddaughter was sleeping over our house one night, and I got to thinking. I must have had a tear or two in my eye as I was tucking her into bed. She looked up at me and said, 'Don't cry, Grandma. My mommy will cry for me.' Hearing that, all I wanted to do was cry. Here's this little girl, who has to deal with so many tests, medications and challenges, worrying about me and how I feel. I'm telling you, she's the best thing our family will ever have. She's always concerned about everyone else and hasn't even once complained about all she has to deal with."

"At first, I thought I could help them."

Tim's Story:

"I used to play basketball after work at the rec center on Monday nights. While I waited for my team to arrive, I watched a team of teenagers playing on the court. This group appeared to have special needs. One player who caught my eye appeared to be in good shape and could run fast. But he had a lot of trouble making a basket, even though he was nearly as tall as the rim. I kept asking myself, 'How did I get so lucky to be healthy and blessed with the abilities I have? Why am I not as happy as that tall kid, who cheers and smiles, even when he misses a shot?' He was happy and determined, he never gave up. Watching these kids made me want to help them. I felt like I should contribute to their team rather than watching them from the bench. I finally mustered the courage to ask if I could help coach. A few weeks later, they invited me to do just that.

I can't believe it's been six years already. Now it's clear they've helped me more than I've helped them. They've made me realize that I put limits on myself in what I could accomplish at work and school. I realized I quit tasks after failing a few times, telling myself I couldn't be successful.

For years, I focused on my frustration and small things that bothered me instead of pushing forward. They inspire me to be determined, kind and grateful. They remind me to take on a positive attitude with my job, relationships and personal goals. I'm the happiest I am all week when I'm driving home after coaching this group. I used to believe that God put me on that bench to notice that these kids needed help. I no longer believe that. Now I believe that God put me on that bench because I needed help to learn about myself. They are my coaches. They demonstrate perfectly how to play your heart out without excuses and without giving up. I'm so grateful."

"Brad's world? Who's Brad?"

Mrs. Henderson's Story:

"I teach art at the high school. Art's an elective class; therefore, most students are motivated and skilled, and plan to pursue art in college. For the most part, students in the special education program don't take art classes. However, one day, I received a call from the mother of a student named Brad.

I knew of Brad and, for the past three years, had seen him in the hallways. But I never interacted with him. He doesn't speak. I'm told he has a Speak Pad, but very rarely uses it. He appears pleasant, quiet, robotic, unexpressive and isolated from others. When Brad's mother asked if he could include some of his sketches and paintings in the high school art show, I said yes, although I was a bit surprised. She explained that he paints and draws at home instead of watching television.

I'll never forget the night of the show. Brad's art consisted of striking paintings, sketches of people and places, and a weaving made of string, buttons and rubber bands that were playful and beautiful. Parents and high school students gathered in front of his work. They took pictures and admired Brad's artistic talent. Many times I heard students and parents asking, 'Who's Brad?' Throughout the night, many students were intrigued and enlightened, and they wanted to get to know him. It was amazing that a person who doesn't speak or express outwardly had so much to say and so much in common with them.

Brad's unspoken words were heard loud and clear through the sketches and paintings of his world, illustrated so clearly with bold, beautiful colors. He sat near his art board that night as students approached him, each one giving him a high-five or shaking his hand. I could see his eyes light up. He seemed happy and understood that they accepted him as an artist. Brad certainly answered the question, 'Who's Brad?'"

My Thoughts: People who don't have a child with special needs—or any children at all—often ask what they should say to parents like me. The short answer: Anything good. Kind words of support and praise are immeasurably beneficial. Our kids will notice when you notice their wonderful qualities.

"Once I understood, I understood."

Justin's Story (age 14):

"My locker was next to Tim's at the middle school. Tim lives two houses down from me, but we didn't hang out. One day, a teacher came into our classroom to do an experiment. Our class met with the kids in Tim's class to see what it was like to have special needs for an entire day. I'd never done anything like this before. Some of us had to spend the day in a wheelchair. Others were blindfolded or wore gloves, earplugs or other things that made it hard to speak, hear, see or get around at school. It was shocking. I was so frustrated because I couldn't do things and everything seemed so hard. Tim and the other kids with special needs helped us. I was asked to write a paragraph on the computer. Sounds easy, right? It was anything but. I had cellophane over my eyes and my vision was blurry. And the gloves over my hands made it impossible to type fast. Tim and his classmates were at the computer station with a few of my classmates and me, trying to encourage us. They told us to take is slow, try again and don't give up. I kept thinking to myself, 'Tim is encouraging me?' For some reason, I couldn't envision him encouraging others. I always saw him as the one needing encouragement. It took me 30 minutes to type a paragraph that normally would've taken me five minutes.

This experience stayed not only with me, but a lot of my friends as well. We all realized how much strength, courage, determination and persistence these kids have all day, every day. But what surprised me the most is they're just like my friends and me. At lunch, we talked about movies, the president, the weather, sports teams and Internet gaming.

One kid even showed me how to work my phone better. He had to show me several times because I could hardly see or work my phone with Saran Wrap over my eyes and gloves on my hands. I was trying not to cry I was so frustrated. From then on, I understood how alike we all are and how strong kids with special needs have to be. Before this, I just didn't know. Well, I knew, but I didn't realize. Tim and I are now friends. We sit at lunch together with his friends and mine. I'm embarrassed to say I wouldn't have understood any of this without that one class."

My Thoughts: Not everyone will embrace our values or those we love. Give others a chance at kindness. It's their choice. If they turn away, move forward toward those who choose differently. Every battle is not worth the fight.

"I love her more than anything."

Nico's Story (age 19):

"I'm away from home for my first year of college. My little sister has a lot of special needs. My parents take good care of us, especially her. I believe in myself. I know I can do and learn almost anything I choose in life because I'm smart. I make friends easily and I have goals. But my sister has taught me everything I really need to know. In fact, she has taught me what most people take a lifetime to learn. Things like how to be kind, knowing how to pick your battles and the importance of determination, never giving up on something just because it didn't work out the first time. It's like she was born knowing what's important.

She's happy and excited about life. And wherever she goes, she shows everyone what real happiness looks like. She hugs me, makes me drawings and cuts pictures out of magazines she thinks I'll like. She doesn't complain or start talking about herself first in a conversation. Instead, she'll ask how you're doing, and she cares about what you say. Sometimes I want her to get better. And, of course, I wish she didn't have to deal with all the challenges of another surgery, test or hospital stay. But sometimes I don't want her to get better. I know that sounds wrong, but I don't want her to change. She's too good to wish she were different."

My Thoughts: Brothers and sisters of children with special needs are like everyone else, with one big exception: They have a front-row seat to the everyday realities of life with special needs. We can all learn from these siblings' acceptance and resilience.

"Trevor took the time to really help me."

Terri's Story (age 17):

"I was in the culinary arts program at the high school and my 16-year-old brother, Trevor, has special needs. He goes to another school that helps him more because of his wheelchair and limited speech. I'm always helping him around the house. Sometimes I get frustrated because, if my parents are going out, I have to stay home with him.

One day, I was trying out new recipes for potpies. I had to create six different varieties for class. Trevor asked me if he could eat some of them. I was happy about that because I don't like potpies at all. Trevor ended up being my taste-tester. He sat with me all day, telling me which ones were too sweet, too salty or just plain bad. We laughed so much that day. Each pie was small, like a cupcake. Sometimes he'd ask to eat the whole pie and other times he'd spit it out. I made a talking board for him. It allowed him to tell me what I needed to add and leave out of the recipes. I realized that Trevor needed a sense of purpose. He had a chance to help someone else, instead of being the one getting help. We named the pies together, and he was so proud and happy that day. I was, too, because he took so much time tasting and helping me adjust the recipes. Now, we make one or two kinds together, and he loves the potpie we named 'Trevor.'"

My Thoughts: Many teenagers willingly embrace our children with their kindness and friendship. Some even risk being misundertood or rejected by their peers. As a group, they are powerful advocates for our children. As individuals, they are irreplaceable and priceless.

"RETARD is a bad word."

Joe's Story (age 9):

"My older brother, Jeffrey, has a hard time talking and playing sports. When we shoot basketballs outside, he can do it. But the rim needs to be lower because, while he has a strong arm, he has just one. My friends are nice to him, but some of the kids his age aren't so nice. When they're not, they don't give him the ball. And sometimes, they tell him to watch instead. Once they get to know him, they're nicer. I don't like when they call him a retard. I tell them they say that word because they judge Jeffrey based only on what they see on the outside. But I know what Jeffrey looks like on the inside. I tell the kids Jeffrey has regular feelings and he should get to play. My mom says some kids just don't understand. I think there are kids with special needs, and there are regular kids, like me, who play with them. The other kids are in the 'learning group' and don't understand that kids like Jeffrey are regular, too."

My Thoughts: You can either echo what the group says to be accepted or speak your mind and risk retaliation. Why not go solo? It's a choice to be a voice, not an echo.

"A lot of things about this are good."

Rosie's Story (age 16):

"Three years ago, Jimmy, a boy I liked at school, asked me to go to the rec center. He wanted me to participate in a social group with kids who have special needs to see if I could help out. I was nervous and hesitant, and I asked myself, 'What do I say to them? 'How can I help them if they don't even know me?'

Since I liked Jimmy, I decided to go. The first thing I noticed is that these kids were happy to be there. They wanted to learn everything, and they listened to directions during the art session and basketball game. After a while, I realized these kids were just like me. Many of them were my age and I became their friend. It's a different kind of friendship because I feel like I'm really important. I enjoyed talking with them. I remember one kid saying, 'Making friends is not hard.' This bothered me for a few days because I knew this boy didn't have any friends at school. A few days later, I asked him what he meant by that. He said, 'Well, making friends isn't real hard. It's real, real hard.'

After that, I started to understand him better and realized he's hesitant, at times, to say what's on his mind. Another teenager told me that getting made fun of by others at school 'breaks your spirit of wanting to be at school and learn.' I didn't realize how much being made fun of distracted her from learning and concentrating at school. It was sad. The one question I'll never forget came from a teenage girl, who asked me if I thought she was stupid.

I was surprised and said, 'No. Why would you think that?' She replied, 'Because my speech is slow, the other kids treat me like I'm stupid.' She demonstrated how she used to talk to show me how she has improved over the years. I remember the tears rolling down my face.

I realized that these kids have real feelings and are aware of how others act toward them, even when they don't say it. They notice good things about others. They don't act entitled or demanding, and they don't hold grudges against others. Being their friend is easy. They don't put each other down or engage in needless arguments. Our friendship has made me a more patient and grateful person. Three years ago, I was their helper. Now they're my friends."

7 Embracing the Good and Those Who Care *A Look Back*

Many brothers, sisters and countless others gravitate toward children with special needs, willingly integrating our amazing kids into their lives. They choose to spend time getting to know these children as individuals, regardless of their disabilities. Quickly, they find that their own lives are enriched by the relationships they form with our children. Our children teach us to see life from their unique perspective.

In time, we all come to realize how much children with special needs can inspire and connect with others on more levels than we could ever imagine.

"From what we sometimes do not understand comes the greatest of passion and genuine affection."
—*Jim Trakas, Member, Ohio House*
of Representatives 1999-2006

Reflections

I'D LIKE TO BEGIN THE FINAL CHAPTER with one undeniably true statement: **Our kids are amazing.**

When you think about how much they accomplish, learn and thrive—given the many challenges they face on a daily basis—they enrich our lives and the lives of those who get to know them.

Only individuals who get to know our children may realize the 9-year-old at the mall with the cute curly hair is wearing a wig. Those who haven't won't realize the intense chemotherapy she received as an infant will prevent her from ever growing hair. Likewise, only those who get to know the teenager who works at the coffee shop will understand the stress he'll feel next week. That's when he'll have his braces removed for the eighth time so he can undergo another brain scan to see if the tumor is growing again.

It's perfectly OK that not everyone knows the medical histories of our children. And frankly, this information isn't everyone's business. However, when others don't understand our children's circumstances or challenges—and no effort is made to get to know these kids—they're often misunderstood, bullied or criticized because of their differences.

As parents and caregivers, we know that prejudging or mistreating our children is a *choice* the other person makes. Collectively, we know that many others will choose differently. They'll choose to be kind and get to know our families and our children for who they are. They'll understand that our children are more like others than they are different. Our children, like every child, have needs. They just have an extra set.

Meeting the demands of that extra set of needs may seem overwhelming for parents and caregivers. But we're not alone in our journeys to figure it out. The hundreds of parents, caregivers, families, coaches, teachers and friends who were interviewed for this book tell their stories to enlighten, even inspire, new parents who find themselves in our shoes. They identify seven truths that form a foundation of resilience, faith and love.

Accepting our situation is the first choice we make. We can let our fear, guilt, grief, uncertainty and sadness immobilize us, or we can use this energy as a springboard to facing future challenges. Accepting that life has changed isn't always easy. The sooner we accept what is, the sooner we can take the first step toward a more fulfilling life. In doing so, we open the door to what we learn about ourselves. We're almost forced to realize our strengths of intuition, tenacity, patience and courage. When we're unsure about what to do next, we realize we have the perfect teachers: our children. Our children give us the answers we need to take the next step. With every turn, they guide and teach us about their world, our world and what's important.

As we witness our children's extraordinary challenges, we begin to see life through a different lens—the New Normal—and focus on what our children can and can't do today. They demonstrate that *can'ts* are temporary, and tomorrow may be another opportunity to witness amazing accomplishments. As our children grow, many of us may feel alone, misunderstood and stuck on the "what if" questions. But we're never really alone. There are millions of us who know what it's like to walk in your shoes. Some walk ahead of us, and some follow. But we all get it. We understand our need to connect with others, especially our partners. By walking this journey as a couple, we unite our strength and courage. We can clearly see that our situations aren't bad, just different. Of course, not everyone will try to understand. And a small group of insensitive, mean, dismissive and intolerant people may even choose to say or do incredibly hurtful things.

As I interviewed people for this book, I heard remarkable stories that made us laugh and cry. Not surprisingly, the emotional pain caused by the insensitive and intolerant doesn't seem to dull over time. We all seem to have this experience. You will too. I like to think of these awkward moments in a positive light and consider them lessons. Some people will choose to learn from us and follow our positive leads, and some won't.

Fortunately, a much larger group loves our children and really cares. They get to know our children. And they learn from them by not simply accepting them, but by embracing them. These good-hearted folks become better versions of themselves for giving our children a much-deserved chance.

Despite our love and resolve, almost every one of us has struggled with the thought that this challenge is just too big. Everyone interviewed agreed that watching a child who's hurting can be unbearable. And many times, the experience reveals to us who in our lives can support us and who can't. Almost every one of us has asked the question, "Will I outlive my child or will my child outlive me?" Parents and caregivers seem to universally understand the question and find comfort in preparing for the answers in either direction. It's a part of the reality that forms our bond.

I describe this journey as trying to solve a giant jigsaw puzzle without getting to see the picture on the box. So how do we figure out what pieces go where without clues? Eventually, we learn that when our intuition begs us to listen, we listen. Sometimes the clues to where the pieces fit were right there in front of us. Combining our intuition with what our children tell us will help connect the pieces. Take comfort in knowing that, through it all, your child will demonstrate strength, courage and love that know no limits.

Regardless of whether you're at the beginning, middle or end of your journey, you're not alone. You understand how life and your perspective have changed. You've come to realize that our New Normal is ongoing, not simply a two-week prescription for an antibiotic. You get how miracles don't go unnoticed and that small accomplishments call for big celebrations.

Life can be filled with more joy and love than we could've ever hoped or wished for. That's a choice we all make.

Your choice is totally up to you.

Contributors

Michael Cioffi
Professional Copywriting and Editing Services
www.mightymonkey.com

Sandra Delaportis, M.D.
Internist at the Cleveland Clinic
www.clevelandclinic.org

Chris DiAlfredi
Chief Creative Officer of Eques—Smart Brand Positioning
www.equesgroup.net

Cindi DiGeronimo
Affiliated with the Corner Stone of Hope
www.cornerstoneofhope.org

Mark Fogliette, D.O
The Cosmetic Surgery Institute of Northeast, Ohio
www.allnewyou.com

Roman Jakubowycz
Business Strategist, Speaker and Podcast Host
www.kinshipology.com

Mark Kalina, Jr.
The Mark Kalina Jr. Foundation provides support to traumatic
injury victims.
www.mkjrfoundation.org

Marcus Marinelli
Owner of Strong Style Mixed Martial Arts and Training Center in
Independence, Ohio
www.strongstyle.com

Jason Marvin
Sergeant Marvin is President of the Ohio Police Juvenile Officers' Association (OPJOA) and Co-Owner of J&N Corporation.
www.opjoa.com

Deanna O'Donnell, JD
Parma, Ohio Municipal Court Judge
www.parmamunicourt.org

Krista Ruggerio
Professional Make-up Artist
ruggles167@gmail.com

Amir Saleem
Founder and Chief Executive Officer of "Blab-On-Air" radio studio for kids ages 7 through 18
www.blabonair.com

Cheryl Taras, CPT
Certified personal trainer/coach and expert in sports conditioning and fitness
xrsize@sbcglobal.net

Kim Taylor
Special Education Intervention Specialist
Brecksville-Broadview Heights City Schools
taylorchr@gmail.com

Jim Trakas
Member, Ohio House of Representatives, 1999-2006
Chairman and Chief Executive Officer of the American Online Learning Center
www.americanolc.com

Beth Tupa
Owner of App2Tapp and Charity Bank Games
www.app2tapp.com | www.charitybankgames.com

Tom Tupa
Former NFL Pro Bowler, Punter and Quarterback
Owner of App2Tapp and Charity Bank Games
www.app2tapp.com | www.charitybankgames.com

Diane VanNostran
Owner of DVN Photography
www.dvnphotography.com

Steve Vojvodich
Co-founder of C-Dox Marketing and Apparel
www.c-doxmarketing.com

John Zakel Jr.
Director of Special Olympics Young Athletes of Cleveland
www.youngathletescleveland.com